I Was Bo [illegible]

Christmas Day:

90s Christmas Telly from Ant and Dec to Zig and Zag

Ben Baker

First published in Great Britain in 2020

By Ben Baker Books

with revisions on this edition in 2021

Cover designed by Paul Abbott (@pablovich)

Produced using Lulu Press.

Find me on Twitter @Benbakerbooks

For Shona and Sarah without whom this book, nor I, would probably exist.

Foreword

Just so you know this is a book that doesn't exist. I didn't write it and I'm sorry if this affects your enjoyment of it.

THE END.

...okay, maybe not. But after writing last year's "Christmas Was Better In The 80s" I'd convinced myself that I had absolutely exhausted the topic of festive telly. Sure, there was still plenty from the seventies I could consider but my lack of being born in that decade would prove a hindrance on the personal context front. And as for the nineties, a decade where I was rarely far away from a blaring convex screen but didn't seem to have an identity, what sort of idiot would try to write about that...?

And then 2020 happened.

Suddenly my regular life of home-office laptop bashing and trying to make sense of the world was becoming everybody's 'new normal' and bar those amazing humans on the frontline keeping things going, most of us responded to these strange new days with a mixture of bellowing into the void, cheap strong lager and a nightly retreat into the comforting nostalgia of old movies and telly. For me, it was YouTube clips where forgotten stars in Day-Glo clothing could stand less than two feet from an audience and cough openly into their faces without so much as a vaguely written warning statement on some green and yellow signage. As I continued to watch, it occurred to me that my soul was becoming wistful for the weird middle ground that the 1990s represented. A time where mobile phones, the internet and DVDs were becoming an affordable reality yet co-existed in a world where Bamboozle on Teletext, the Funfax and VHS cassette labels marked in red ink "MUM'S TAPE – SOLDIER SOLDIER – DO NOT TOUCH" were still a regular sight in many homes.

Programmes like "Bad Influence" and "The Net" used to tease an astonishing technological future (with a name like the 3DO, how could it possibly be bad!) as late night programmes like "Clive James on Television" and "Manhattan Cable" opened the stained velvet curtains to a wider world of telly – all of it cheap, invariably bonkers and / or featuring a parade of nude bums. Arbiters of taste and culture railed against these changes and warned that more television would actually be a bad thing for us and that these new companies wouldn't be able to sustain the quality of the traditional terrestrial channels. Pah, as if.

Depending on your point of view my family got lucky in August 1990 when we managed to get Sky satellite television installed. And by 'installed' I mean some random bloke my Dad knew came round to the house with a second hand dish and receiver box. Back then Sky only charged for their two movie channels and I quickly realised that you could baffle the box into unscrambling its bounty by wiggling the card about until it gave in and let us see Chevy Chase in "Funny Farm" or whatever cinematic treat was previously hidden to us. Despite the quality of the programmes, which were often held together by dust and sadness, I'm exceptionally nostalgic for those pre-Simpsons days where the peak was WWF highlights and "Sky Star Search", a Keith

Chegwin-hosted talent show almost identical to "Britain's Got Talent" except for the sets, viewers, drama, spectacle and talent.

At the start of the nineties terrestrial telly was still where all the actually good stuff lived with no shortage of drama, comedy, quiz and light entertainment formats to drag in the viewers; even if it did mean you might end up seeing duelling David Jasons on several channels at once. As I entered my pre-teens BBC2 and Channel 4 were rich playgrounds of interesting ideas, new faces, challenging concepts and comedy that felt totally different to anything that came before, much of it influenced by the speed at which the decade hurtled on. And yet along the way something went wrong. Maybe it was the all-encompassing millennium on the horizon or the uncertain times that would come with the expensive switch to digital television and its initial audience that could fit in a Mini Metro with plenty of leg room to spare. Others might blame the deregulation which meant households no longer had to buy both the Radio and TV Times leading to the rise of the cheapo no-frills magazines like What's On TV[1], TV Quick[2], TV Right Bleedin' Fast, TV Too Late You Just Missed It and TV Much Slower Now After The Pills, Doctor flooding the newsagents' shelves.

For some it went wrong when devious bidding wars designed by

---

[1] Still the country's second biggest selling magazine with weekly sales of 765,392 behind relative newcomer TV Choice which launched in 1999. The nearly five times more expensive Radio Times comes in 5th with average sales around 283,366 whilst the TV Times is 17th averaging 118,718 a week. All data according to ABC circulation figures as of February 2020.

[2] Which ran until a very respectable mid-2010. The others may be a lie.

the outgoing Thatcher government meant many favourite ITV regions – including Thames, TVS and even TV-am - went off air as December 1992 became January 1993. Executives eventually realised it was cheaper to point a camera at members of the public rather than take a risk on untested new programming. BBC Two and Channel 4 became obsessed with the food, property market and renovation culture that to this day still dominates the schedules of both, whereas BBC One and ITV seemed to struggle to find new plans to find the next "Only Fools And Horses" or "Inspector Morse" and even the few new hits of the time were soon besieged by copycat programmes, often on the same channel. And for many it was when Channel 5….well, just Channel 5 really.

And yet despite all that has changed, we still come together at Christmas. Granted in 2020 it might be via one of those big bubble things John Travolta wore in that film or shouting to Uncle Pat that he's on mute every three minutes but nevertheless, the seasonal period remains the one time a year everyone still makes the effort and spends time with the people they love. And it this year it means being able to watch the box without an elderly relative muttering every ten minutes "telly was better in my day", "bring back The Del Boy!" and "when's Hardwicke House on?" then so be it…

Therefore this book doesn't exist. And as such we won't be going for a well-deserved nostalgic paddle in the past as we try to swim away from the suspicious brown log in the whirlpool tsunami that is 2020. Roll the tape.

Ben Baker, 37 feet below Seabase, The Bunker, Up Tarn.

1990

Highest Rated Programme: Soaps all the way with "EastEnders" beating "Coronation Street" by a whisker (20.17 million viewers to Corrie's 20.16m.) In second place for both BBC One and ITV were these new-fangled Australian types with 18.30m tuning in for "Neighbours" and relative newcomer "Home and Away" managing to pull over 15 million. Over on BBC Two "The Witches Of Eastwick" would top the ratings with five and a half million whilst comedy dominated Channel 4's ratings with Tommy Cooper compilation "Just Like That" doing the best business (4.29m).

Big Films on the BBC: A double bill of Dennis Quaid is naturally what most households expect around this time of year and 1990 delivered the premieres of sci-fi comedy "Inner Space" on BBC One and thriller "The Big Easy" over on Two. Other premieres included the enjoyably daft "Spaceballs", eerie Jim Henson adventure "The Dark Crystal", rotten He-Man adaptation "Masters of the Universe", vampire fantasy "The Lost Boys" and weirdly despondent kids flick "Flight Of The Navigator". For the big Christmas Day movie, BBC One greeted the first appearance on the small screen for 1982's "E.T: The Extra Terrestrial" right after the Queen. Less inspiring was the lacklustre Diane Keaton 1987 comedy "Baby Boom" which took up the 9:45pm slot.

On variety alone, BBC Two undeniably won for film premieres with the first TV broadcast of Claude Berri's two part saga "Jean De Florette" and "Manon des Sources", Tim Burton's massively fun debut "Pee-Wee's Big Adventure" and the sequel documentary to "Koyaanisqatsi", 1988's "Powaqqatsi" all sharing space. Although they also had the best forgotten - for all reasons -

1986 box office disaster “Roman Polanski’s Pirates” so y’know… ehh. Fans of men in barely knacker-covering animal furs could also thrill to a season of 1930’s and 40’s Tarzan movies each morning on BBC Two and BBC One bigged up their acquisition of the brown tod-looking thing from space with a season of Spielberg movies.

Big Films on ITV: An underwhelming choice to go against “E.T” with the 1979 Bond film “Moonraker” getting its third festive run out in under a decade. The powder was instead kept dry for “Beverly Hills Cop II” later that night which saw over 12 and a half million settle down for another ‘specially ruined for television’ adventure with Axel Foley. On subsequent evenings the punters flocked in for “Dirty Dancing” and its natural successor “My Left Foot”. The Disney Vault finally coughed up the UK TV premiere of the always upsetting “Pinocchio” on December 22nd. It also gave us “Splash, Too” and the horrific “Return to Oz” but nobody asked for that. Except perhaps child psychologists.

Big Films on Channel 4: No huge blockbuster movie premieres but there’s a selection of WC Fields classics during the afternoons and Jonathan Ross introducing some late-night Cantonese fantasy movies including the brilliantly titled 1980 Sammo Hung martial arts horror “Encounters of the Spooky Kind”.

Oh That Queen’s Speech: Queen Elizabeth “paid tribute to the role of the armed services in the context of imminent war in the Persian Gulf” which feels a bit like a sneak preview for 1991’s new season. Hope there’s a new series of “Boon” too…

For The Kids: A fairly mixed selection on BBC One with the traditional new series of "Why Don't You?" joined by sub-Muppet antics from Germany in "Hallo Spencer", creepy magic peculiarity "Wizbit" and the diabolical "Popeye and Son". ITV kept it relatively simple with "The New Adventures of He-Man" and lots of boring live action films that nobody has managed to get round to watching on Disney+. If that all sounds too gripping, Channel 4 had the serialised 1949 "Batman and Robin" shorts and "Tintin".

The Pops: As many have been reminded by the recent BBC Four "Top of the Pops" repeats 1990 was an eclectic and often damn fine year for music. So it's a shame that most of that was bypassed in favour of Status Quo, Bombalurina and Bloody Cliff Richard. Thank Jebu for Adamski, Kylie, Beats International and The Beautiful South then! Sadly an earlier timeslot meant a clash with Channel 4 showing Lisa Stansfield in concert from 1pm! ITV had at least spent their own wad with a big musical contribution at 8am via… oh… "The Cliff Richard Christmas Day Special" which promised songs[3], "the Christmas story", "clips from his latest tour" and Cliff "introduces the Choirboy of the Year". No. BBC Two later found space for Amnesty concert "An Embrace of Hope" from Chile. Alas it did not feature 90s rockers Embrace or Bob Hope on the bill. Even more unusual was the scheduled "Toto – Live in Paris" concert on BBC One late Boxing Day considering they hadn't had a UK hit since 1982.

---

[3] Cliff was Christmas No.1 that year with "Saviour's Day" thus depriving the country of the previous week's No.1 "Ice Ice Baby" at the top of the Christmas pops. Meanwhile in Ireland, they had Zig and Zag…

Radio Times Cover: A mildly sinister painted tableau of Santa watching the telly as a young girl clings on to his chest in admiration while a big plate of mince pies are proffered by what appears to be a young Nick Knuckle from "Palace Hill". Santa is more transfixed by the chunky video recorder on top of the TV which would probably bring a nice few bob down the boozer come Boxing Day. This would be the last RT to sell over ten million copies (10,601,244 to be exact) as new deregulation meant people no needed to buy two double issues. Boo. £1.10.

TV Times Cover: More plump Santa fun as "Coronation Street" actresses Helen Worth and Sally Whittaker loom large in red outfits to somewhat crassly promote the fact both are playing characters who are "in the Christmas Pudding Club!" or pregnant if you don't speak tabloid bollockese. Anyway…spoilers and that but Sally's going to have Rosie in the back of a taxi on Christmas Eve whereas Gail has to wait until the following day to pipe out future bad boy David. There's also room for a small picture of the much missed Ken Dodd, presumably to frighten any children into brushing their teeth after a full selection box. Price is also a reasonable £1.10.

New Year's Daze: A straight forward wry sideways look back at the year with "Clive James on 1990" at 11pm followed by ten minutes of chimes and cheering then it's up to "Carry On England" to start the new year off for BBC One. Much more rock and roll on the sister channel with a concert by those 'faces of the 90s' The Rolling Stones recorded that June up the Barcelona.

ITV spared no expense with "Live from The London Palladium. Happy Birthday, Happy New Year!" one of those slick, spectacular and a depressingly soulless shows celebrating 80 years of the beloved variety theatre. Doing their turn on the famous stage was a truly mystifying mix of "today's stars" - including Jim Dale, Bea Arthur, Michael Ball, Bobby Davro, Andrew O'Connor and Gary Wilmot - paying tribute to "heroes of yesteryear" who are too dead to complain about it.

The real quality light entertainment however was over at Channel 4 with the nineties first comedy sensation…and singer Vic Reeves who welcomes us to his "New Year's Eve Big Night Out" which made a rare concession to celebrity guests including Mark Wingett from ITV's long-running police serial "The Bill" interrogating Reeves over his dodgy businesses and a rigged "Top Pop Singer of The Year Contest" featuring Kim Wilde and "Male Pop Star" - actually Michael Starke, better known as Sinbad from Brookside. ("It's Large!") A brilliant half an hour of television frustratingly left off the 'complete' series DVD of "Vic Reeves' Big Night Out" released in 2005. This was followed by concert films featuring the spirit levels of pop Squeeze (yay!) and the soil in which chives grow UB40 (boo!)

Theme Nights: One of the greatest on New Year's Day courtesy of Channel 4's "1001 Nights of TV" hosted by Michael Palin featuring "three hours of bizarre, powerful, off-the-wall and unashamedly nostalgic extracts plundered from the archives".

Wouldn't Happen Now: I mean we get as far as page four of the Radio Times before an appearance from "Sir James Savile" showing off his new chair "designed by the Cybernetics Department at Reading University". I'm sure they're thrilled now. BBC One had the daily series of "Paddles Up" (paddles up what?) which saw people doing stuff in canoes - an idea that I suspect wouldn't fly today despite its impressive run between 1983 and 1993.

New For '91: Starting on the BBC on January 3rd were two comedy shows of varying infamy with "The Brittas Empire" and "The Mary Whitehouse Experience" although "Gordon The Gopher", also, new that day could take the lot of 'em. In contrast ITV launched "The $64,000 Question", "Beverly Hills 90210" and erm..."Spatz".

Is The Sound Of Music On? No. But the TV Times has a useful guide on how you can become a "Dirty Dancer". Naturally I put my foot through the sixties and sent Patrick Swayze's ghost the bill.

Saturday, 22nd December, 1990

1.10pm: Saint and Greavsie (ITV)

"In today's edition, Ian St John and Jimmy Greaves preview tomorrow's clash between Aston Villa and Arsenal"

Not the most auspicious a beginning to the book you might think but the light 'banter and balls' of this Saturday afternoon staple featuring an couple of ex-footballer pundits is an interesting place to stick the thermometer of where the world was at this precise time in the 90s. Initial fun comes right out of the gate as the real Jimmy is too ill to come to the studio and so has been replaced instead by his "Spitting Image" puppet voiced by former ITV commentator Peter Brackley [4].

The recent extraordinary unification of East and West Germany is covered in a piece by Jim Rosenthal from a heavily snowed over Stuttgart where a new amalgamated German team were about to play for the first time in nearly 50 years. Despite being a light piece for a football preview show wedged between "The Chart Show" and Dickie Davies' "Sportsmasters", there's a thoughtfulness given to the subject and the slightly depressing thought that bringing together the two formerly separate zones might raise problems when attempting to form under one sporting banner. Especially when comparing the German Democratic Republic where the government believed "sport is not private amusement, it

---

[4] Best known to a generation of gamers as the voice of "Pro Evolution Soccer". Greavsie's usual voice actor Steve Coogan presumably being otherwise engaged.

is social and patriotic education"[5] with the more affluent, European-influenced 1990 World Cup winners West Germany's dominance in the sport. The answers would take some time to emerge on the International side however few former East German teams have thrived in the combined National leagues to the despair of many a football fan.

A more comic item investigates the new 'art' of celebrating a goal in an elaborate way – something hugely common in modern times - which many had been introduced to by Cameroon's Roger Miller with his cheeky flag dancing moves during the World Cup. There's also a report from England and Derby County goalkeeper Peter Shilton's Testimonial friendly match featuring an "Italia '90" squad vs. England stars of past[6], present and a "man for the future" – the 22-year-old Matt Le Tissier who would go onto have a slightly complicated history with the national squad through the decade. After a hot and happy summer of England actually being quite good at the World Cup and even having a decent single in New Order's "World in Motion", the team were still very much being seen as heroes. Sadly, it'd be the last time for a few years as the Graham Taylor-era of doom saw no wins at Euro '92 and the total failure of the team to make the World Cup in 1994. The most striking thing of all with this edition of "Saint and Greavsie" though is the amount of football they had to show. Sky Sports

---

[5] The oft repeated motto of "sportfuhrer" Manfred Eward (1926-2002), the GDR's Minister for Sport from 1961 to 1988. A former Hitler Youth, he was later convicted for his role in a state sponsored doping of East German athletes competing in the Olympics.

[6] A goal coming from the then-39 year old Kevin Keegan, a decade before he'd take the manager's job.

would not exist for another four months yet soon its unprecedented £304m bid for coverage of the new Premier League would kick start both the rise of the Sky's big money successes and the struggles of the terrestrial channels to compete, a sadly predictable story which has continued ever since.

And with no football to show guess which punditry double act got the axe? Poor ol' Saint and Greavsie. It's a funny old wossname.

Sunday, 23rd December, 1990

5.30pm: Bullseye Christmas Special (ITV)

"This afternoon's Bullseye has a Dickensian theme with host Jim Bowen as Scrooge and a host of celebrity guests."

More ITV sport? Have I gone quite mad? Well, yes, many years ago but this Christmas edition of the beloved Sunday afternoon staple is worth talking about simply for how baffling it is. As the blurb suggests, Bowen is indeed in full Ebenezer Scrooge garb and railing miserably at both the audience and the celebrity guests who are also in full costume. As its 1990 Bobby Davro is Bob Cratchit, Bella Emberg his wife and Paul Shane essays a not very tiny Tiny Tim. Some Santa-hooded 'ghost' dartsmen Leighton Rees, Eric Bristow and Bob Anderson are also there to throw them arrows and of course Tony Green is dressed as Jacob Marley. What follows is a frankly surreal half hour as everyone attempts to stay in character but also play the game for real. With it being for charity, there are a lot of bulls-eyes thrown as the celebs answer the questions. There's room for Davro to do his impressions including a lengthy section as Bowen himself and Emberg is the butt of some dire fat jokes much as she always seemed to be back then. Most mesmerising of all is Paul Shane who looks half dead with biscuits round his mouth yet clearly also really wants to win and only breaks character at the very end.

The topic of festive "Bullseye" is always one that resonates with me as the year following this special my parents decided to treat us to Christmas in a fancy hotel where the star turn on the big day was no less than Jim Bowen himself. To say he had some Scrooge-like qualities of his own was no understatement as he struggled to run a punter-based game of the darts favourite before giving up in a huff. Not the most professional behaviour but the copious booze the guests had been knocking back since breakfast probably had something to do with that…

Monday, 24th December, 1990

9.35am: Charlie's Christmas Project (BBC One)

"…All he wanted was to look after a dog called Arfie."

A Canadian children's drama from 1984 notable for being one of the most depressing half hours ever broadcast on TV (homeless dogs on death row...) and the title character being played by a ten year old Seth Green. The episode was taken from the hammer-over-the-head moralistic anthology series "Young People's Specials" which also featured editions entitled "Grandma Didn't Wave Back", "Zerk The Jerk", "That Funny Fat Kid", "Narc" and "My Father the Clown".

Monday, 24th December, 1990

9.30pm Madonna in Concert (BBC Two)

"In August 1990 Madonna's 'Blond Ambition' tour reached Barcelona."

10.50pm: The Fabulous Singlettes (BBC Two)

"It is 1962, and in a dingy flat in London's Earls Court, three Australian girls pine for home."

11.25pm: This Is Spinal Tap (BBC Two)

"A rockumentary by Marti DiBergi…"

Madonna leads the charge after perhaps the biggest year of her career which had begun with "Dear Jessie" still riding high in the charts before new single "Vogue" became a sensation all over the world. That song and follow up No.2 hit "Hanky Panky" would feature on an accompanying soundtrack for the new blockbuster Disney film "Dick Tracy" in which she also had a major role as Breathless Mahoney. After a highly publicised fling with her co-star Warren Beatty and the filthy "Justify My Love" video, November saw the colossal selling "The Immaculate Collection" best of compilation released just in time to become the biggest album that Christmas[7]. How she managed to fit in a worldwide tour between all that gawd knows but here she was with a huge dance troupe, lavish stage production and, famously, costumes by

[7] It is currently the 20th highest selling album in the world of all time and has charted consistently in the UK, last appearing in the way back year of August 2020. Or 'two months ago' at the time I'm writing this.

Jean Paul Gaultier, not to mention a documentary crew making "In Bed with Madonna" but that's way off in 1991…

Formed in 1986 by Naomi Eyers with Alison Jiear and Simone Dee, The Fabulous Singlettes had quickly become a sensation with their mix of girl group hits and catty humour being named "Pick of the Fringe" by the BBC and nominated for an Olivier Award in 1988. Appearances on everything from "Michael Barrymore's Saturday Night Out" to "The Children's Royal Variety Performance" followed within 18 months culminating in their own Channel 4 variety hour on Boxing Day 1989. Whereas that had been a straightforward recording of their live act, "The Fabulous Singlettes" was an unusual half hour that attempted to mix the stage act with a period sitcom not dissimilar to what "Flight of The Conchords" would do years later. Full of striking set design and great period detail which tapped into the love of all things pre-Beatle that the UK was going through thanks to films like "La Bamba" and "Dirty Dancing", "Unchained Melody" hitting No.1 for a month and endless "Happy Days" repeats, it's a bit of a strange beast overall with screeching gear shifts in mood. One sequence features the trio suddenly breaking a scene for a beautiful but melancholic a capella rendition of "Teen Angel" played completely straight. Even the audience giggle nervously, confusing the genuine oddness of those 1950s novelty hits for deliberate gags.

Despite a good script by future "Ed Reardon" co-creator Andrew Nickolds and comedy legend Geoff Posner at the helm, this was the last the world would see of the three piece for a time after Naomi Eyers left the act in 1991. The strange scheduling probably didn't help matters but it's a testament to BBC Two's much missed experimental nature that it was even commissioned in the first place.

More period pop followed with the always joyful heavy metal pastiche “This Is Spinal Tap” which was just creeping out of cult infamy onto a wider stage that would eventually result in a Tap revival in 1992 with a new album “Break Like The Wind” and a memorable Simpsons guest appearance in “The Otto Show” where Christopher Guest and Michael McKean joined regular cast member Harry Shearer for a disastrous live appearance in Springfield. After all that, viewers might be expecting an exploding piano or miniature St. Stephens Cathedral as “Brendel Plays Schubert” closes out this Christmas Eve. Sadly it’s just a bloke called Brendel. Playing some Schubert. It’s very nice though. Could use a smoke machine…

Tuesday, 25th December, 1990

11:45am: The Famous Teddy Z (BBC Two)

“Teddy and Laurie are ordered to stay in the office on Christmas Day.”

A slightly earlier slot than the 9pm engagement the first six editions of this forgotten US sitcom were gifted the previous October. It's easy to see why BBC Two had been enthused – here was a new celebrity-based show by the creator of “WKRP in Cincinnati” and the first “Police Academy” movie Hugh Wilson and starring Jon Cryer, fresh from “Pretty In Pink” and the admittedly terrible “Superman IV: The Quest for Peace”. Cryer appeared as the title character - a young mailroom intern named

Theodore "Teddy" Zakalokis who talks his way into representing a difficult movie star at a large talent agency. It all seems a little bit far-fetched but the situation for this comedy was actually based on the real life career of MCA clerk Jay Kantor in the 1940s who became Marlon Brando's agent in a similar manner.

Pre-empting the trend for the next two decades, "The Famous Teddy Z" was pulled from air in the US before the end of its first series, with five episodes not shown. BBC Two would have another crack at prime time with five more episodes of the now nearly two year old series in a 9pm slot before quietly moving it to lunchtimes where it vanished just before completing the 20 episode run. Despite its early bath, gravelly-voiced co-star Alex Rocco, best known to British audiences as either Moe in "the Godfather" or the unscrupulous head of Itchy and Scratchy Studios, Roger Meyers Jr., would go on to win the modestly titled 'Outstanding Supporting Actor in a Comedy Series' Emmy in 1990 beating out Kelsey Grammar and Woody Harrelson for "Cheers".

Tuesday, 25th December, 1990

6.25pm: Bruce's Christmas Generation Game (BBC One)

"A fun-packed bumper edition with couples competing for prizes."

A revival of the super-popular 1970s family spectacular with original host Bruce Forsyth at the helm had returned to screens in September 1991 when Bruce returned to the Beeb after a decade away for the bizarre prize-stealing game show "Takeover Bid".

When that didn't gel with viewers the BBC's Head of Light Entertainment Jim Moir suggested they give the old format another crack. Initially going out on Friday nights, the revived series was almost identical to the original and soon built up its audience week by week resulting in 16.73 million looking in here[8] between the famously downbeat "Only Fools and Horses" special "Rodney Come Home" and extra-long episodes of the similarly bittersweet "Bread" and "Birds of a Feather".

A much-needed blast of old school light entertainment with a raft of gags and features that could – and almost certainly did – turn up in the original twenty years only with handbell ringing, the audience being encouraged to "A Bicycle Made For Two", a ballet sketch not dissimilar to the act Forsyth was doing at the London Palladium 35 years prior and everyone gathering round a piano at the end to sing "White Christmas". Not everything works - some of the patter would be a hashtag waiting to happen in the modern age - but it's the games and challenges at the heart of the show that still drive it forward as regular members of the public get the chance to try new things and act hilariously badly alongside cameos from comedian Kenny Lynch, Neighbours' Madge and Harold (Anne Charleston and Ian Smith) and the actual real Captain Birdseye off the adverts.

Forsyth constantly reminds us throughout why he's at the top of his game and it's hard not to grin at daft throwaway lines like *"You design golf courses, jails and hotels…So its links, clinks and 40 winks…"*

---

[8] The only real shame being that ITV put "Ken Dodd Live at the London Palladium" out in almost the same slot, splitting viewers after a bit of lighter non-sitcom fare.

The success of this special meant the "Generation Game" remained at the heart of Christmas schedules for the next few years until Jim Davidson turned up and ruined it. But there'd be more Brucie bonuses on Christmas Day a decade later as "Strictly Come Dancing" became another huge hit in a sixty-year career full of them. Didn't they do right good and that?

Wednesday, 26th December, 1990

6.00pm: Christmas Cluedo (ITV)

"Santa arrives at Arlington Grange with a sackful of surprises for the assembled guests. One has murder in mind…"

Some potential game show formats seem to take forever to come together whereas others can be staring you in the face for decades. Created by Anthony E. Pratt and first manufactured by Waddingtons in 1949, "Cluedo" had been setting generations against each other for…well, generations with its mix of country house gentry, soap opera intrigue and big blunt objects to bray the living snot out of some poor unfortunate victim. Despite a much loved cult 1986 American movie adaptation[9], it wasn't until 1990 that a TV adaptation with famous folk playing the potential murderers made it to air[10]. Changing the cast every series, viewers

---

[9] Simply titled "Clue" and featuring three different endings.

[10] A series with a similar premise but no official licence called "Whodunnit?" had been a successful format between 1972 and 1978 for ITV, hosted in turn by those behemoths of crime Shaw Taylor, Edward Woodward and Jon Pertwee.

would join two celebrity teams to ponder a short film before grilling their wildly improvising suspects.

In this special edition, we're treated to the one-off combination of Ian Lavender as Professor Plum, Kate O'Mara as Mrs Peacock, Toyah Willcox as Miss Scarlett, Joan Sims as Mrs White and Reverend Green played by king of the comedy clergy Derek Nimmo all being unnerved by the arrival of an extremely young and menacing Sean Pertwee. Attempting to crack the case were two people off "The Bill" (Tony Scannell and Trudy Goodwin), an Australian actress presumably here to do panto (Fiona Spence) and actual real-life murderer Leslie Grantham who bizarrely would later join the series in its fourth and final run in 1993 as Colonel Mike Mustard. It's these later, slightly dafter series, hosted respectively by Chris Tarrant[11] and Richard Madeley that readers might remember more as the format played up to its game show leanings. The host for the first series and this special was Dr James Bellini who at the time was more known as a presenter on more serious programme such as Panorama, The Money Programme and Newsnight and is now, according to his website, "a leading futurologist and author with a considerable reputation". And yet it never mentions "Cluedo" once!

Its murder I tells yer!

---

[11] Tarrant famously loathed the job later being quoted as saying "I absolutely hated hosting Cluedo, it's the worst thing I've ever done. It took forever to make the thing. We used to have to turn the studio audience over just to make sure they didn't get any bed sores."

Friday, 28th December, 1990

10.35pm: Arts Review 1990 (ITV)

"The South Bank Show looks back at the best of the arts in 1990."

A programme I post about mainly to go "Cor!" at the contents including "extracts from Stephen Sondheim's musical Into the Woods, John Malkovich, Inspiral Carpets and Bolshoi Ballet star Irek Mukhamedov" 1990 had been a year where pop culture and high culture were closer bedfellows than now with Glasgow becoming the first city in the British Isles to be named "European Capital of Culture"[12], The Stone Roses playing the much-discussed Spike Island gig, the BBC launching Radio 5 - its first new station in decades with a heavy arts and culture remit and the World Cup making Pavarotti's "Nissun Dorma" a No.2 hit in the actual pop charts. Over on the albums chart, "The Essential Pavarotti" would become the first classical album to reach No.1 in the UK, a feat he repeated several months later when "In Concert" recorded live with Placido Domingo and Jose Carreas as "The Three Tenors" also hit the top, eventually going on to be the biggest selling classical album of all time. Granted most of its listeners couldn't tell the difference between "Turandot" and a boil on the bum but it was progress nonetheless and brought opera into more accessible places, like your mum's cassette deck. A timely reminder than ITV was once a leading light when it came to arts programming.

---

[12] England itself wouldn't get the honour until 2008 when Liverpool did us proud. And thanks to You Know What, we'll never get it again…

Tuesday, 1st January, 1991

12.30pm: Going Loco: The Final Puff (Channel 4)

"Channel 4's recent Going Loco season takes to the airwaves again - in concentrated form - bringing together some of the season's highlights to delight buffs and steam widows alike."

Perfectly paced for the pie-eyed person with a banging New Year's headache, this compilation featured the highlights of a Channel 4 theme week from the previous September celebrating 30 years of "continuous steam". The contents were decidedly varied with a four minute drama "Train To Lymington" featuring a tweedy chap with an quirky sense of humour (Christopher Good) having an awkward conversation with an inquisitive teenage girl (Claire Parker) aboard an old fashioned carriage train. There's the brilliantly named "Let's Go To Birmingham" featuring an enormously sped up Strauss-soundtracked 1962 train journey from London's Paddington station to Birmingham's Snow Hill like the BBC used to shove on back whenever there was an awkward gap in the schedule.

For personal reasons, the most interesting item of the bunch is "The Emotive Locomotive", billed as "a wry look at enthusiasts' passion for the iron horse", which features my local Keighley and Worth Valley Railway. From the opening anecdote about a baby accidentally catching fire due to sparks from a train (the baby was fine as the subject in question was telling the story himself) to the aficionado talking about making girls cry when he told them were getting trains "wrong", this is a pleasure from start to finish revealing a world that, despite being only three decades old, feels like a world away. It's one of those brilliant small-scale character documentaries Channel 4 were brilliant at when it was still happy to be unusual and outsider.

Sadly there was no room in the schedule for a repeat of "Steam Sunday", an odd live extravaganza from Horsted Keynes Station in Sussex which had kicked off the "Going Loco" season originally. Helmed by the tiresome Mike Read in full Partridge mode the special featured a scattershot collection of guests braving the terrible weather including Sam Brown and her dad Joe, Jools Holland, Miles Kington and Instant Sunshine, Pete Waterman, famed locomotive artist David Shepherd and the cast of "the Railway Children" reunited, including the mighty Cribbins. Astonishingly the awkward mix of live blues music, deafening horns and diesel engine chat doesn't quite get the pulse racing but I urge every reader to find it, especially performance poet John Hegley singing his anthem "Trainspotters" on the platform to the genuine bewilderment of passing punters in horrendous sweaters.

Tuesday, 1st January, 1991

8.30pm: Happy Feet (BBC One)

"The pupils of the Dora Jackson School of Dancing compete in the 1960 Classical Dance Festival in Scarborough. Fifties rock 'n' roll meets classical ballet with the arrival of Dora's ex-boyfriend and a mysterious ghost."

Not them there animated penguins; this was a Screen One special by Mike Bradwell set in the early 60s. The big hair, the pursed lips from bickering old ladies and stolen glances between lovers is purest "Coronation Street" as we follow a group of young dancers and their families through a seaside talent contest. More a series of vignettes than a focused story, the setting and cross-talk of pushy mothers, awkward teenage boys and small-time dignitaries occasionally feels like an extended Victoria Wood sketch. There's even a Jim Broadbent in a cameo as a grumpy grocer. It's a lot of fun with a good eye for character and Britain before The Beatles came along and kicked off the sixties properly. However if you're just into seeing people off of "Lovejoy", Phyllis Logan (Lady Jane) and Chris Jury (Eric) are in the cast, 'Joyfans! Erm…joy!

Tuesday, 1st January, 1991

10.55pm: The Hangover Show (BBC Two)

"A hilarious monologue on the pains and pleasures of alcohol."

A funny and sincerely fascinating comic talk performed by the late Pete McCarthy. Previously one of those faces that cropped up on TV a lot including work with his own troupe The Cliffhanger Theatre on sci-fi pastiche "They Came From Somewhere Else" and police sitcom "Morning Sarge". Co-written with fellow stand up John Dowie, this show saw the amiable everyman McCarthy come to the foreground with this adaptation of his 1990 Perrier-nominated Edinburgh show about the fun and unfortunateness of getting hammered. Perfectly timed for New Year's Day, the levels of drinking are investigated in painful but funny detail from stage one's first drink of the day to stage six's blackout *("why be hidebound by social conventions? Hands and knees are a perfectly acceptable way to get to the toilet…still feeling good, still feeling convivial, unfortunately you've just been sick on somebody else's shoes..."*) with real scientific descriptions of why hangovers happen and the chemical tango going on instead your brain. Cures from around the world are suggested albeit offered with caution (*"Doctors? How can anyone take ex medical students seriously!?"*) A particularly brilliant running joke sees McCarthy quoting from the grim 1972 tome "Kingsley Amis on Drink" (*"Kingsley Amis...famous for hating two things in the world - women and everything else"*) leading to an unfortunate end.

A huge hit at the time, this would prove to be the breakthrough for McCarthy who would go on to a very successful career in presenting travel programmes (Channel 4's "Travelog" and "Desperately Seeking Something" among them) and writing, with both of his books -"McCarthy's Bar" (1998) and "The Road To McCarthy" (2002) - becoming best sellers. Sadly his success would be cut short by his far too early death from cancer in 2004 aged just 53. Raise a glass to a genuine one-off, my friends.

1991

Highest Rated Programme: The fairly underwhelming two-part "Only Fools and Horses" special "Miami Twice" dominated both Christmas Eve and Day although the former comfortably came top with 17.7 million again the second instalment's 14.9 million viewers. ITV's main hit was as per "Coronation Street" with 13.69m. The biggest show of the whole Christmas period wouldn't come until the 29th when the first ever "Aunties Bloomers" cleaned up with 18.24 million watching Wogan introduce clips from engineers' Christmas party blooper tapes with all the swearing and bosoms cut out.

Big Films on the BBC: A good year for comedy on BBC One with "Scrooged" and "Planes, Trains and Automobiles" specially cut to ribbons for pre-watershed viewing as would be the Tim Burton "Batman" which took pride of place on Christmas Day at 6pm bringing in 14.30m viewers. At least they had the good sense to save Eddie Murphy's raucous "Coming to America" until later in the evening. Elsewhere "Rain Man", "A Fish Called Wanda" and Steven Spielberg's oddly forgotten "Empire Of The Sun" raise up the high scores whilst Michael Jackson's "Moonwalker", "The Great Outdoors" and a "Howard: a New Breed of Hero" bring them back down again.

BBC2 also has a Spielberg premiere to itself – "The Color Purple" which appears as part of a mixed bag of first runs including "Platoon" and Branagh's "Henry V". There are also nightly musical movies with Chuck Berry ("Hail! Hail! Rock 'N' Roll"), Tom Waits ("Bigtime"), John Lennon ("Imagine") and the premiere of Talking Heads' joyful "Stop Making Sense" concert film from 1984.

Big Films on ITV: ITV's Christmas is oddly muted with more old favourites and ropey TV movies than new releases BUT there is room for two - yes TWO! - "Police Academy" premieres with 1987's "Citizens On Patrol" on Christmas night and the following year's "Assignment Miami Beach" three days later. What a time to be alive! The third channel also had a rare season of late night films as "Rear Window" starts an always welcome run of Hitchcock classics.

Big Films on Channel 4: Still transitioning from their interesting arty beginnings into the dull mass of nothing they are these days, 1991 saw an unusual amalgam of first airings including 1942's "The Reluctant Dragon", entertaining Anthony Horowitz-penned kids crime spoof "Just Ask For Diamond" and "Monty Python Live At The Hollywood Bowl". There's also room for a run of post-midnight Jackie Chan films just as he was starting to make a name for himself outside of Hong Kong cinema.

Oh That Queen's Speech: It must be weird being the Queen and seeing the world suddenly change massively just as you hit regular retirement age. 1991 was a big year for upheaval and Liz found time to mention the "enormous changes taking place across Eastern Europe and Russia". While the Isle of Man gets nothing as ever!

For The Kids: A very random mix of repeats on BBC One including "Defenders of the Earth", "Pingu", "Poddington Peas", the near thirty years old "Touché Turtle", Oliver Postgate's post-"Bagpuss" 1984 series "Tottie: The Story of a Doll's House" and sodding "Lassie". More "He-Man" and third tier Disney films on ITV including "Escape to Witch Mountain" and "That Darn Cat". Slightly more interesting was "Cosgrove Hall's Box of Crackers" featuring some of the beloved animation studio's one-off specials. And for those kids with access to a satellite dish, The Children's Channel was now running for a positively crazy 13 hours a day after previously being limited to four.

The Pops: "Top of The Pops" is back in its comfortable 2pm slot but – oh no, it's that dreadful Year Zero period where no-one was allowed to mime and only the most forgettable hosts could do the job hence Mark Franklin, Tony Dortie and Claudia Simon presenting here. For a year dominated by that dreary record breaker from "Robin Hood: Prince of Thieves", and a re-issued 1975 single fronted by a dead man the mix of guests in the studio is…interesting to say the least. Attempting to represent the now live dance hits in the studio are 2 Unlimited, Oceanic, Erasure, Nomad ft. M.C. Mikee Freedom and Seal with James, Right Said Fred, Chesney Hawkes and The Scorpions trying not to look like acts already past their biggest hits. As for Kenny Thomas, I think he represents…bins?

Radio Times Cover: More Santa but a ruddy faced close up this time and no endangered children. He does however have a copy of that very same Radio Times in his mitts for a bit of Christopher Nolan style recursive mind-bendage. Sales are down to 4.8 million yet the cover price remains a handsome £1.10.

TV Times Cover: It's the breakout stars of 1991 – TV's Larkin family from "The Darling Buds of May" – David Jason, Catherine Zeta-Jones, Pam Ferris and that other bloke showing us how to "have a perfick Christmas!" There's also a chance to win three family holidays to Australia and 'His 'N' Hers Vauxhalls'. And all for a quid!

New Year's Daze: 1991 saw BBC One sticking with the familiar Clive James end of the year spectacular – now extended to 90 minutes - before a brief check in with Big Ben and a message from the 'Archbish'. Presumably this is to save time getting to the late movie "National Lampoon's Movie Madness", a film that can be best described as…..on once. BBC Two stick with cinema too but offers the excellent double bill of "Mad Max" and "This Is Spinal Tap". ITV also put in the minimum effort with a brief New Year break between parts of 1986's "Down And Out in Beverly Hills". Channel 4 easily put the most elbow grease in with "As It Happens" an 'as live' fly on the wall documentary reflecting Moscow's first "free" New Year.

Theme Nights: BBC Two's delightful "A Perfect Christmas" on December 21st filled the schedule for over twelve hours starting with "The Flowerpot Men" and "Dr Finlay's Casebook" before bursting into colour with the Den and Angie divorce papers episode of "EastEnders" and the now slightly verboten "Top of The Pops" from Christmas 1973. After some archive Queen, a surprisingly rare showing of "It's A Wonderful Life" which had made its BBC debut on Christmas Eve 1957 after which it had been shown by the corporation just ten times in four decades and almost never at Christmas. Later on Morecambe and Wise,

Steptoe and Son and famous ghost story "The Signalman" nestle beside lesser-seen picks such as 1964's variety show "Christmas Night With The Stars", a 1980 documentary about Strangeways prison at Christmas, Jack Rosenthal's 1975 play "Evacuees" and new compilation "A Stocking Full of Christmas Clichés" looking back at television traditions. This schedule was a big part of developing my love for archive TV and it remains testament to how good BBC Two was around this period.

Wouldn't Happen Now: There's no "EastEnders" on Christmas Day. Not a scrap. None. Zero. Not even so much as a Cockney rolling down a hill on fire! And why? Well, it was a Wednesday! And "EastEnders" don't do Wednesdays!

New For '92: After a whole seven years away, the cast of "Are You Being Served?" returned in the thankfully more subtle "Grace and Favour" as the characters took over the running of a country hotel. There was also new comedy drama with Keith Barron and Nigel Havers in totally forgotten "The Good Guys" and "Moon and Son", a strange but fun murder mystery series by the legendary writer Robert Banks Stewart starring Millicent Martin as a crime solving clairvoyant. None of them went beyond two series.

Is The Sound Of Music On? I'm afraid not.

Wednesday, 18th December, 1991

7.30pm: Tomorrow's World Christmas Quiz (BBC One)

"Will the studio audience be able to outwit James Burke and his panel of experts in separating fact from fiction?"

A constant on BBC One from 1967 to 2003, "Tomorrow's World" was the average person's window into what was happening in science and technology with fairly straight-laced tests of new products or inventions which, as many a parody of the show pointed out, wouldn't be in the shops for flippin' ages. The incorporation of a more playful quiz format come late December wouldn't be introduced until 1986 with the team's older brother-type Howard Stableford as host. The tone would be set by his increasingly disagreeable seasonal jumpers and a series of groaner jokes ("*You know a lot about nuclear physics...I'll try not to 'fall out' with you then...*") generally absent from the usual episodes .An always pleasant change the quiz saw the audience taking on a panel headed up by a less obvious celebrity such as "Hitchhiker's Guide" author Douglas Adams, David Bellamy and not one but two Doctors Who (Whom?) - Colin Baker in 1986 and Sylvester McCoy in 1988, both in full costume. They'd be joined two professionals from the scientific or medical worlds. Here former 70's "Tomorrow's World" host James Burke was joined by Professor Lesley Rees and Dr John Hassard.

The central premise of the quiz remained more or less the same throughout the run - here's a thing and here's three different possibilities about what it might do - an example in this episode being a leather strap which is suggested to be an hot air balloon 'holder downer', a didgeridoo holder or an easy hay bale grabber. To show off the gadgets would be the regular team which at this point consisted of Judith Hann, Maggie Philbin, Carmen Pryce, Kate Bellingham and the late Times journalist John Diamond.

Like most of its light entertainment schedule mates, there was plenty of room for more celebrities to pop on and shill their latest project with the biggest name here being an extremely uncomfortable David McCallum accompanied by a panto horse as promotion for the unpopular BBC horse racing drama "Trainer". Later there's the cast of the live "Thunderbirds" stage show and Paul Merton, still very much a cult name at the time, clutching a stuffed sheep. The finale of the 1991 show was incredibly of its time as Burke and "audience champion" Anneka Rice took on each other in those old school virtual reality machines with the big chunky helmets. The graphics, showing the two trying to turn each other into frogs, are perhaps laughable thirty years on but you can still get the sense of excitement that era of gaming advancements was for pre-teen gonks like me who had already progressed from the Atari 2600 to the Amiga.

Despite its cheesy presentation and stilted conversation in places, its hard to dislike this with a feel not dissimilar to teachers putting on a show and letting their hair down at the end of term. Sadly, the 1992 edition of the Quiz was to be its last with the final "Tomorrow's World" as a whole coming in 2003. It's hard to say whether technology began moving too fast for audiences to continue being to be excited about anymore or the constantly-updating internet made us more cynical to new developments. But this is certainly a format that deserves another shot.

Sunday, 22nd December, 1991

7.30pm: The Goodies Christmas Special (Comedy Channel)

Despite the generic title, this sadly wasn't a new adventure for the Superchaps Three who had ridden off into the sunset after a wobbly series on LWT in 1982 but a showing of the classic "The Goodies Rule - OK?" from 1975. Perhaps the most ambitious episode of the series, the double-length episode begins as a spoof on pop stardom and ends with the trio being attacked by TV puppets including the giant Dougal and Zebedee from "The Magic Roundabout". But why was a fifteen year old BBC show cropping up on a Sky Channel hardly anyone had?

To answer that we have to jump back to several years earlier and the announcement of BSB - British Satellite Broadcasting - a UK based competitor to the growing Sky franchise. It had been a hard fought battle for who should get the licence with five major bids going forward in 1986 backed by the varying likes of LWT, Dixons, Goldcrest Films, Saatchi and Saatchi, the American chain Sears and, of particular note to this story, Rupert Murdoch's News International who, upon losing their bid, decided to build upon a stake they had in the existing "Sky Channel". It would take four years and an eye-watering amount of money to launch but BSB made it air with five brand new channels in March 1990. By this point, Sky had been up and running over a year even if its content was pretty much crappy sitcom repeats, American game shows and programmes imported from Murdoch's US station Fox. BSB would represent quality and range both in programming and their more expensive equipment.

This was still the Wild West days of satellite TV with jokes about its crapness on every comedy show and very few willing subscribers. BSB launched with a huge advertising campaign and a notable square aerial receiver promising arts, music, movies, sport and entertainment. Of course, there were plenty of repeats on BSB too and you could regularly find the likes of "Hart To Hart" or "Mr Ed" next door to "Till Death Us Do Part". "Steptoe and Son" and "Doctor Who"[13] thanks to its partnerships with the BBC and various American companies. "The Goodies" had also been a regular presence on the channel which was of great excitement to fans that hadn't had a sniff of a trandem in years. These scarcer repeats were one of the main pulls for people opting for the 'squarial' company in an era still a few years away from UK Gold or any real archive TV output. Sadly the money ran out before hauling in enough paying viewers with conscientious customers hanging back to see which of the services would thrive. Alas, you probably know how the rest of this story goes: a merger of Sky and BSB was quickly drafted into place with "British Sky Broadcasting" or "BSkyB" becoming the new joint name in November 1990 - an arrangement that would surprisingly last until 2014.

Now the only game in town Sky had access to most of BSB's programme library and would poach many of its American imports for Sky One. The other stuff went on "The Comedy Channel" - launched on 1st October 1991 to show even more rotten old US sitcoms but now with "Porridge" and "The Young

---

[13] The channel devoted a whole weekend of rarely seen Doctor Who episodes, including incomplete rarities, that September which is still the prized possession of many a fan.

Ones" next to superb Canadian sketch comedy series "The Kids in the Hall", Australia's top rated "The Comedy Company" and various stand up showcases. To add insult to the whole thing, the station was encrypted and only available to those with a subscription to one of Sky's movie channels which many disgruntled BSB viewers stuck with the service didn't even have. This would last just a year but thankfully by then UK Gold was just around the corner and with nightly Goodies repeats to boot. Not to mention a whole new set of problems…

Sunday, 22nd December, 1991

8.15pm: British Comedy Awards (ITV)

"Jonathan Ross hosts live coverage of the second annual British Comedy Awards."

It's probably indicative of the cliquey boozy do boredom that the "British Comedy Awards" became in its later years that you saw this listing and immediately thought of arrogant actors saying the F word and insulting their disabled producers. Yet those early years were legitimately a thrill to see for comedy spods like myself with strange people from weird sketch shows suddenly turning up on a respectable ITV programme in Christmas week. In fact, it was so respectable at first that the initial ceremony was hosted by borin' ol' Michael Parkinson and featured gongs for Roy Hudd, Russ Abbot and Jean Boht from "Bread".

It was this second year with Ross now the new host when the event started to become a slightly more alternative affair. ITV may seem strange these days as a venue for such a show but this was a time where it was still showing odd, satirical and rude comedy, often in a Sunday 10pm timeslot. Not that any of their shows get a sniff as Clive Anderson, "Have I Got News for You" and Vic and Bob were the big names on the night. Even the weirdly branded "Best ITV /C4 Comedy" went to Channel 4's newsroom newcomer "Drop The Dead Donkey". There was still room for some older favourites with Beryl Reid getting the "Lifetime Achievement Award" at 72 and a 95 year old George Burns receiving the strange "International Lifetime Achievement Award". Perhaps most exciting of all for what would come to define comedy would be in the frequently ignored category of "Best Radio Comedy" which saw "The Million Pound Radio Show" share the title with Radio Four's serious news magazine programme "On the Hour".

It wasn't the year of Julian Clary's comments about an encounter with the former Chancellor of the Exchequer (1993) or the room-exploding response from Spike Milligan on hearing a letter from Prince Charles (that was 1994) but those moments highlight the "anything can happen" fun those early live broadcasts could be. The ceremony was eventually dropped by ITV after various scandals and sinking viewing figures made it less worth the hassle. Channel 4 had a go for a few more years but the idea of dressing in a tuxedo and clapping politely with your peers seemed to be from a different lifetime ago, an era the "British Comedy Awards" arrived off the back of. Comedians wanted to be rock stars, not thank their agents for the opportunity! But we'll always have grovelling bastards and fisting. If not necessarily in that order…

Monday, 23rd December, 1991

8.00pm: Bernard and the Genie (BBC One)

"Bernard is really looking forward to Christmas - until he gets ditched by his girlfriend and sacked by his exceptionally nasty boss. But when he accidentally conjures up his own deeply funky Genie the tables start turning!"

Few people had lived up to their potential as much as Richard Curtis in the eighties. From writing some of the best sketches on "Not The Nine O'Clock News" to his successful screenplay for "The Tall Guy" with "The Black Adder" and his much more successful ancestors in between. The 90s had started strong too with a mostly silent comedy starring his old mate Rowan Atkinson about a well-meaning, bumbling menace named Bean plus the continued success of Comic Relief alongside one of the few people who could match him for an equally successful 1980s. Lenny Henry had gone from Saturday morning kiddies' favourite to household name with a range of hugely successful comedy shows, many of which had his name in the title. So bringing these two together for a TV movie should result in something very special indeed. And its name was "Bernard and the Genie".

A breezy comic adventure lasting just over an hour, the Bernard of the banner is played by Alan Cumming - at that point fairly unknown outside of the odd Scottish production and being one half of Victor and Barry, a comic lounge act with his partner Forbes Masson. Both would eventually make their name with "The High Life", a gloriously silly BBC Two sitcom in 1995, but for now Cumming was still a bit of "that bloke from things" which slotted perfectly with the naive but optimistic art dealer

Bernard who tries to do the right thing and is beaten by the world for it. Luckily for him there's another character name in those titles and after an unfortunate lamp explosion *("Do I still look vaguely human or have I turned into Julian Lloyd-Webber?"*) he comes face to face with the manic, sword wielding Josephus (Henry) freed from his lamp after 2000 years (*"2000 years? Most of my friends will be dead!"*)

What follows is a unambiguously joyful friendship as the Genie helps Bernard turn his life around while he enjoys the best of the modern world - which in 1991 means going to see "Terminator 2" and eating everything in London ("*I'm glad dog meat is still popular*!", says Josephus walking past a kebab stall) - before disaster strikes courtesy of in the form of Rowan Atkinson playing a brilliantly slimy boss relishing the opportunity to use his full range of vocal tricks ("*That's a fully-fledged BASTARD of a point...*") rolling a "B" in his mouth as if it's a bullet, together with a habit of needlessly saying "ye" in most sentences including the memorable "bugger ye off". Dennis Lill gets a similarly good turn as a loyal but constantly lying doorman ("*I had a friend who had both his legs blown off and he was up and walking around in a fortnight*") who is perhaps Bernard's only true friend.

The special effects are sparingly used considering the BBC budget but still stand up with the opening scene featuring a mad dash through a bazaar looking good enough to be from an Indiana Jones film...albeit one with lines like *"I'm sorry about your daughter....look, it was my first booking as a knife thrower"*. Director Paul Weiland keeps the story moving apace while Curtis turns in one of his best scripts to date with Cumming and Henry both seemingly having a ball alongside some well-chosen cameos from Gary

Lineker. Melvyn Bragg and Bob Geldof, all backed by the always excellent music by Howard Goodall.

With all the hallmarks of a Christmas classic that could run and run it's deeply frustrating that boring rights issues meant it was only shown twice by BBC One. There are traces of the over-sentimentality and good guy fetish that would crop up in the likes of Curtis' later "Love Actually" and "Yesterday" - two films I loathe with a passion - but the jokes are strong and the smile never leaves your face. Truly if there's one grumble with the script itself it's that it could easily be extended to full film length and indeed a big screen version has seemingly been on the cards since this first went out. Mind you, considering Graham Linehan was supposedly co-writing it with Harvey Weinstein attached as a producer maybe it's no great loss...

Monday, 23rd December, 1991

8.00pm: Des O'Connor Tonight (ITV)

"Des O'Connor brings the festivities with comedy and music..."

It's no understatement to say 2020 has been cruel when it comes to deaths and of the higher profile names the worlds of British comedy and light entertainment have taken a huge hit. Few of them could match Des O'Connor for longevity with eight top 30 hits, including the 1968 number 1 "I Pretend", over 25 studio albums and a TV career incorporating hit variety, game and talk shows stretching back to 1963. And yet time doesn't seem to have been kind to the legacy of Des who has become largely unknown to an entire generation bar the odd appearance on the Morecambe and Wise Christmas shows *("If you want me to be a goner, get me an LP by Des O' Connor.", "Des O' Connor is a self-made man...I think it's very good of him to take the blame", "Des - short for desperate!")* sending up his own image. It's a shame as Des was your all round entertainer who didn't really care about getting any deep and meaningful secrets out of the people who he interviewed and that's exactly why they queued up to appear with him.

Starting on BBC Two in 1977 before moving to ITV seven years later where it stayed for nearly two decades, "Des O'Connor Tonight" was perhaps the most successful series of its kind for sheer endurance if nothing more. This was a slick show with the shiniest floors - a light entertainment shop window with Des as the store manager, cracking wise and playing the straight man when required. His was a show after all that become home to a number of comedians before they became megastars including David Letterman, Michael Keaton and Jay Leno – one edition in 1981 featured the mind-melting combination of Jim Davidson, Lena Zavaroni and Garry Shandling. Another had a 27 year old Jerry Seinfeld alongside The Nolans. His patience is tested with his first guest on this 1991 Christmas special - Bernard Manning who starts with a "dolly bird" gag then protests *"I cleaned that one up!"* An unquestionably bright if stubborn soul, the tuxedo-clad Manning looks like a man out of time flitting between crude racial gags and talking proudly about his comedy club and a childhood in the 1930s. It was a strange transition period for Manning whose act was increasingly unsuitable for television yet soon to get a shot in the arm from the straight to VHS market with "Shooting From The Lip" and the spoof sex education video "Banging With

Manning" around the corner. Whether this preaching to the converted nature of a fans-only club set made his act worse is anyone's guess but I'd be fascinated to know if Jackie Mason, the other comedian on this O'Connor bill, had been in earshot when Bernard told his Jewish gags...

Before Mason gets to the stage though it's time for Cathy Dennis to do her No. 25 hit "Everybody Move". It's all too exciting and feels as if some youths have accidentally stormed the stage but luckily for the older folk watching the next singer - a *"girl whooza bin doin well allova da world"* in Des' own words - is much duller. Its Mariah Carey trying to crack the British market which had at that point only offered her one Top Ten single compared to her five US No.1s in a row. Here she performs the song that broke that streak - the soul ballad "Can't Let Go" which would peak at twenty here in the UK. She'd soon become stratospheric with the release of "Music Box" in 1993 but for now she's another turn and she doesn't even have the decency to do "All I Want for Christmas Is You" simply because it won't be written for another three years yet.

The headline act for tonight is the man who put the "light" into "light entertainment" and the "nose" into "jokes about Barry Manilow having a big nose" Mr Barry Manilow. A consummate professional, Manilow performs "Jingle Bells" with as little feel as is possible before a "spontaneous" chat in front of screaming fans. His was another career in a strange place with no real hit singles since 1984 and it'd be another year before Take That's cover of "Could It Be Magic" would spark an interest in his back catalogue. The whole thing concludes with a Des and Baz duet of "White

Christmas" in such a sugary way that even Alan Partridge would turn it down as "a bit much".

This is a chat show before Alan Partridge brought the tropes to light but after Jonathan Ross and Ruby Wax had added a unique spin on what could be done with the genre. Des was unquestionably a unique talent but eschewed a Monkhouse-style reinvention in favour of his comfortable old-school charm even when it felt increasingly out of place on prime-time TV. His enthusiasm never seemed to waver even when moving over to daytime telly before quietly stepping out of the limelight. But then when everyone's racing for the finish line, Des seemed happiest in the middle of the road and judging by the thousands of endearing stories that flooded in after his death, it seems that was how we liked him too.

Tuesday, 24th December, 1991

5.45pm: Father Christmas (Channel 4)

"Father Christmas enjoys a spot of international high life, until it's time to come home for another "blooming" Christmas."

Despite being written five years earlier than the now perennial favourite "The Snowman"[14], it had taken nearly a decade for "Father Christmas" to take its place next to Raymond Briggs' beloved tale of a little boy and his flying frozen water-based

---

[14] This half hour is based on two of Briggs' books: "Father Christmas" and "Father Christmas Goes On Holiday"

acquaintance. It's a much funnier and cheekier film than that thankfully with none of its heart-string tugging. The casting of the much-missed Mel Smith as the title character is an inspired move and he strikes the perfect tone of grumpy but good hearted while he harrumphs and potters through his suburban British house after yet another successful delivery run.

Facing the audience he talks through what he does all year which includes building a flying camper van to take him on a series of holidays including France where none of the food agrees with him (with a series of comical needs to lay a cable), a freezing cold dip in Scotland and getting cleaned out by a casino in Las Vegas. After that it's time to go through the children's letters to gauge the presents needed before its time to get off again, crawling through chimneys and getting caught on TV aerials on Christmas Eve. The animation is as gorgeous as its predecessor, particularly as Father Christmas fights his way through the snow. A brief dream sequence where the big man is haunted by monstrous versions of the food he's eaten is also wonderfully odd. He even finds time to make it to the famous snowman's party as seen in the earlier Briggs animation. *"Glad you could make it again...the party, not yer snowman!"* says our jolly hero rather casually as if he's not retro-fitting a happier ending to "The Snowman" after nearly a decade of tears!

There's no Aled Jones this time but Smith – no stranger to the festive hit thanks to "Rockin' Around the Christmas Tree" in 1987 - himself sings the jolly title song "Another Blooming Christmas" which cannily had also been released as a single that year. Being as the programme it was from hadn't been shown yet however, it failed to catch on and stalled at No.59 in the Official Charts[15]. Despite getting his famous costume from the dry cleaners and having a whole lorry of letters addressed to "Father Christmas" arriving at his door, the outside world seems generally happy to turn a blind eye to his real identity. There's no Mrs Christmas, no elves or help of any kind that we see, just his reindeer and beloved cat and dog but it's not a sad life portrayed but one of dedication and self-appreciation. And with a sherry in hand and the word "bloomin'"[16] never far from his lips, his is a life well lived.

Tuesday, 24th December, 1991

6.30pm: Big Break - Celebrity Christmas Special (BBC One)

"Jim Davidson welcomes celebrity contestants the glamorous Linda Lusardi, Jean Alexander and entertainer Charlie Drake."

Another Christmas special for an unexpected hit that hadn't existed the previous December; "Big Break" was a snooker-based game show that should not have worked in the slightest but was annoyingly watchable. Annoying because at the helm of the show was Jim Davidson, another comedian I find it very hard not to judge by…well, everything he's ever said or done. He works well

---

[15] A slightly more successful commercial venture featuring the character would be an advert for "Kit Kat" produced in 2006. Reworking the opening scene to feature the titular chocolate bar is well animated if a bit tacky.

[16] A sanctified U.S. edit apparently exists with all the "bloomin"s removed and Mel Smith replaced by William Dennis Hunt who IMDB tells me is best known as Emperor Wang the Perverted in "Flesh Gordon" (1974)

here though around the monosyllabic John Virgo and the "characters" of snooker. Indeed it's surprising to learn that he wasn't even the intended host as an unaired pilot had been filmed in May 1990 with Cockney shouting man Mike Reid as the host, assisted by John Parrott. Deciding it hadn't worked but having built the set, they figured they'd let Davidson have a go and stick it out low key during Christmas. The recording went well and it was decided to rework it as the first episode of a twelve part series where it quickly caught on hanging around ultimately until 2002.

This first special would be a regular half hour with added costumes and celebrity guests including Charlie Drake with whom Davidson had previously worked in panto with. In fact both were in the one proper pantomime I saw as a kid – "Cinderella" at the Bradford Alhambra in 1989. Clearly it gave Jim ideas as not long after "Big Break" gave his career a boost he'd go on to produce his own 'blue' version of the story titled… "Sinderella" co-starring once again with Charlie Drake. Please promise me you'll never ever watch it.

Wednesday, 25th December, 1991

2.50pm: Coronation Street (ITV)

"Alma Sedgewick and Ken Barlow have seldom had happy times at Christmas. Will this year be the exception?"

An unusual experiment for the Street here with the episode beginning at the rather unusual Christmas Day time of ten to three aka 'just before The Queen'. However this was no anarchic statement from Percy Sugden's ghost to smash the monarchy as the speech was worked into the plot with Alf and Audrey Roberts sitting down to watch 'er Majesty before the action continued. And what action it was! Well, alright not compared to the usual terrorist hijackings and murders of present soaps but some characters were certainly behaving in a way which would not be appreciated by others! The main drama centres on Alma and her ex Mike Baldwin who pops round unexpectedly for a chat and maybe....a shag? At this point, her character was in relationship with Mike's eternal nemesis Ken Barlow who is clueless to the rampant rumpo taking place across the road. There's also room for a bit of comedy as constant losers in life Curly and Reg decide to nip into their own supermarket after hours for some supplies before the latter gets his collar felt by the fuzz.

It's all very low stakes with lots of good character dialogue, mostly in the Rovers Return. Sadly we're denied the opportunity of Alf Roberts commenting on the Bond film scheduled after or "The Truman Show"-style possibility of him turning on ITV and seeing himself staring back on the screen. You can have that one for free Charlie Brooker!

Wednesday, 25th December, 1991

5.55pm: This Is Your Life (ITV)

"Michael Aspel prepares to make Christmas truly unforgettable."

A regular face on British TV since the fifties, David Berglas, the magician and mentalist was perhaps a slightly less glamorous star than some might have expected from a rare Christmas Day edition of "This Is Your Life". Only eight episodes were aired on the 25th with the first being the 88-year old former military hospital matron Isabella Woodford in 1961 with a thirteen year gap before Arthur Askey received his second big red book. Muhammad Ali (1978), Eric Sykes (1979), foster mother Joan Wells (1980), soprano Kiri Te Kanawa (1981) and Les Dawson (1992) being the only other members of this exclusive club. Still, despite the fact that Berglas might not be the most exciting recipient, be thankful it wasn't the guest whose edition aired the following week: one G. Glitter Esq.

Wednesday, 25th December, 1991

10.05pm: The Ghosts of Oxford Street (Channel 4)

"Malcolm McLaren directs an extraordinary musical film which charts the little-known history of one of the most famous shopping streets in the world."

In a worryingly prescient opening for the year 2020, the former Sex Pistols manager McLaren, mask wearing and miserable, stumbles around in the shadows as jazz music plays. He decides a Christmas Masquerade ball for the dead is in order at the site of a former ballroom and, before you know it, Alison Limerick is here with a techno theme song to celebrate "magic" being "back". That's about as much plot as is required from this typically high concept piece by the 44-year-old and yet oddly timeless McLaren who monologues about London's darker side and his favourite subject - himself[17] - in amongst appearances from the hippest pop

[17] John Pickard from "2 Point 4 Children" plays a Bet Lynch-wigged young Malcolm in a sailor suit at one point.

acts of the era. To set the tone, Malcolm talks about the weekly Monday hangings that once occurred where Marble Arch now stands over a re-enactment of some jailed rogues in a horse-drawn vehicle winding its way to the nooses. Providing the soundtrack is the Happy Mondays' cover of the Bee Gees' "Staying Alive". As the condemned men are led from their cage we get to see they are in fact being played by the Happy Mondays themselves with Shaun cast as highwayman Jack Sheppard. Tom Jones is up next as department store magnate Gordon Selfridge, before and after success before Rebel MC does some of 'the rap' in the back of a Jeep. There's a surprising turn by Nasty Nick Cotton (or John Altman if you'd prefer) as opium addict Thomas De Quincey haunted by visions of Sinead O'Connor.

The appearance of those we've lost, including performance artist Leigh Bowery and the astonishing Kirsty MacColl as courtesan Kitty Fisher is oddly comforting as is the fact Shane MacGowan is still astonishingly alive. The latter two do that song with the problematic words in that we've all heard enough but it's almost welcome in this cod-Victorian setting. A gorgeous looking film, directed by McLaren himself with a dreamlike quality, is the sort of thing Channel 4 was brilliant at – a mixture of high and pop culture that doesn't take itself too seriously. The "I was best at being outsider" tone from Malcolm might wear on some viewers but then again, with the extraordinary life he led, who can truly claim similar?

Sunday, 29th December, 1991

7.15pm: Auntie's Bloomers (BBC One)

"For the very first time, Terry Wogan sweeps up a collection of calamities from the cutting-room"

Picture it. A scene from one of your favourite TV shows. You know what comes next; you might even know the lines. And then suddenly something goes wrong - a prop breaks, a timed effect doesn't work or, more often than not, the actor completely forgets what they're going to say next. It's exciting, something new you haven't seen before and generally very funny. This was the selling point of "It'll Be Alright on the Night", hosted by comedy writer Denis Norden for ITV between 1977 and 2006, which collated "bloopers" from various TV and film productions for audiences up to 20 million. Actors even began to say "one for Denis Norden!" when caught messing up a take.

Despite this rival success, the BBC were very slow to get in on the act. A series of audio clangers ("Can I Take That Again?" hosted by Jonathan Hewat) would appear in 1982 but viewers would be limited to "The Golden Egg Awards", a short section on Noel Edmonds' "The Late, Late Breakfast Show" (1982-86) where one of the people featured fouling up would be given a comedy trophy. So there was both excitement and apprehension for "Auntie's Bloomers", a collection of BBC-based blunders hosted by Terry Wogan, sourced from both the National and Local arms of the Corporation known affectionately by many as "Auntie Beeb". The result was the highest audience of Christmas week with over 18 million viewers checking in for a mix of classic clips from “Nationwide” and “The Young Ones” next to newer shows such as “Challenge Anneka” and “The Detectives”.

Made initially by Celador before the BBC took over themselves, the picture quality of some of the clips was often a little ropey and eagle eyed viewers will have spotted various things either blurred or blocked out on screen throughout. These were 'fluffs' snipped from what has commonly been referred to as “Christmas Tapes” - videos made by the back room technical staff for their end of year boozy bashes. Initially quite gentle and jolly, the content had got naughtier as the technology improved and a standard video would feature a mix of outtakes, messages from off-duty celebs, out of context clips, sketches and song parodies often done by the engineers themselves. Oh and boobs...lots and lots of nude boobs. This was for a 1970s Christmas do after all and there was a tacit understanding the recordings would be available for staff eyes only. Predictably one escaped and the BBC's first full tape “White Powder Christmas” was eventually seen by an outraged Sunday People (“ANNE TELLY SPOOF SHOCK FOR BBC”) thanks to a fairly tame re-edited bit of tape making it look like Princess Anne was talking about sex.

The news of this tape did little to bother the public but soon a war between TV companies would break out for who could compile the most titillating tape. The BBC continued in 1979 with “Good King Memorex” which raised the game thanks to the stars now knowing what the engineers were up to leading to the peculiar sight of Suzi Quatro singing a parody of her own recent single “She's in Love with You”, improvised sketches featuring John Cleese and Tom Baker on the set of the Doctor Who story “City of Death” and Jimmy Savile...well let’s just leave that one there.

Despite many frequently sexist and cringeworthy segments, the tapes are fascinating documents of the times they were made with less image-conscious famous folk and BBC TV Centre seeming like a constant whirr of activity. After a decade of cuddly Denis Norden and now the nation's half-cut uncle Terry Wogan at the helm, seeing comedy cock-ups with un-bleeped swearing, occasional on-set raging and no audience laughter gives the contents an eerie, almost forbidden feel. Later series of "Auntie's Bloomers" would play up to this "contraband" feel with a title sequence showing a midnight raid on BBC TV Centre to steal the tapes and a 007-aping Wogan presenting the show supposedly from the "bowels of the Beeb" surrounded by film reels. With the success of this first show it was perhaps surprising that the "Bloomers" would not be promoted to the Christmas Day schedules until 1995 with yearly new editions making it to air usually just after the main celebrations. Sparing with new editions at first, production suddenly into overdrive from 1997 with four new shows including a wildlife-specific episode in July. From there we had three in 1998, three in 1999 and a whopping fourteen in 2000 before it came to an end in Christmas 2001, being replaced the much less interesting "Outtake TV".

The Christmas tapes were undoubtedly of their time but highlighted then-current out-takes which are now beloved such as Simon Groom admiring "a beautiful pair of knockers" on "Blue Peter" and new unseen moments from shows we've known forever such as "Fawlty Towers", "The Goodies" and "The Two Ronnies". Admittedly they also gave us sexism, racism and that bloody swearing "Rainbow" thing with Tommy Boyd and Jim Davidson. But we'll always have "MERRY CHRISTMAS VT!"

1992

Highest Rated Programme: Another brutalizing by the BBC who took more than half the available audience for all but one programme in prime-time ("The Generation Game" which just lost out to "Coronation Street") There can only be one champ and that was once again "Only Fools and Horses" and the episode "Mother Nature's Son" which saw 20.13 million viewers get a taste for Peckham Spring. Top rated movie would be "Indiana Jones and The Last Crusade" with 15.80 million viewers seeing how the trilogy ended. And it did end. There was no fourth film. No.

Big Films on the BBC: The only movie worth talking about is Weird Al's "UHF" which found its way to BBC One in the excellent time slot of 11:45pm on December 21st. But I could mention Willy Russell's wonderful 1989 comedy "Shirley Valentine" easing out Christmas night to the delight of 13.86 million viewers. Elsewhere, there's space for premieres of the rumpo-laden "Sea Of Love", "Twins", "When Harry Met Sally" and the sappy Spielberg-backed "The Land Before Time" which at 69 minutes should barely qualify for this section. "Women on the Verge of a Nervous Breakdown" launched BBC Two's Christmas with "Dangerous Liaisons", "The Fabulous Baker Boys". "Monty Python and The Holy Grail" and "Earth Girls Are Easy" keeping the quality high, along with another Hitchcock season.

Big Films on ITV: I mean, what you're really asking is "when is "Mac and Me" on?" The answer is December 22nd. Hope this helps! Another woeful line-up of films from the third channel with a mystifying Christmas Day double bill of Martin Short and Nick Nolte comedy crime vehicle "Three Fugitives" (1989) and ice hockey drama "Youngblood" (1986) which probably made the cut due to starring a pre-fame Rob Lowe and Patrick Swayze.

Big Films on Channel 4: A TV movie version of "A Connecticut Yankee In King Arthur's Court" with Rudy from "The Cosby Show? Where do I sign?!? Compilations of Chaplin shorts appear on the run up to Christmas followed by a Sidney Poitier season. Also making an appearance late night are a number of films by Chaplin and Poitier's equal cinematic legend Godzilla with the lesser seen "Ebirah, Horror of the Deep" followed by 1967's "Son of Godzilla" and "Destroy All Monsters".

Oh That Queen's Speech: Not a banner year for Her Majesty. In fact, it was the one about the 'horrible anus' (annus horribilis, surely?) thanks to Windsor Castle catching fire, all the divorces, Fergie's topless toe-sucking, Andrew Morton's tell-all book about Diana and "Squidgygate", a series of intimate conversations "somehow" taped between Diana and her friend James Gilbey.

For The Kids: Philippa Forrester and Toby Anstis introduce a less cartoon-heavy line-up on BBC One than usual with "Why Don't You?" returning and Tony Robinson telling religious stories in "Herod's Christmas" - a spin-off from an obscure Sunday morning series named "Blood and Honey" that most kids will have slept through – along with a second repeat of the 1982 Australian drama "Come Midnight Monday" which features that age old tale of teenagers fighting a local businessman to stop a steam train being decommissioned. Cartoon-wise there are repeats of "Swamp Thing", "Babar" and the deeply ironically titled "The All New Yogi Bear Show". ITV are still going with "He-Man" and rotten old live-action Disney movies like "Pollyanna" and "The Three Lives of Thomasina".

The Pops: Another dire year for the UK chart with only 12 new records managing to hit the top and singles sales at a crashing low. But Mark Franklin and Tony Dortie try to put on a brave face as they introduce some of the blandest songs of the decade including Wet Wet Wet's "Goodnight Girl", "Please Don't Go" by KWS and Undercover's dire cover of "Baker Street". Still, Shanice and Jimmy Nail are on hand with everyone's favourite Bradford-born chanteuse Tasmin Archer ~~Badger~~. Nothing else on a pop tip that day but later BBC Two had the quirky compilation "Reindeer Rock" while Channel 4 showed a "tribute to the music of Bob Dylan" featuring Eric Clapton and Ian Mellencamp's dad, John.

Radio Times Cover: A small girl creeps behind a hollow eyed snowman - I mean they're all hollow-eyed admittedly but this one is at least sporting a natty red Radio Times logo scarf - but, yeah… someone gonna die. Also: "over 500 movies!" £1.10.

TV Times Cover: More snow monstrosities! At least it's a jollier snowman having been visited by a Scotty dog, some birds and a cat which - I do not exaggerate – is seconds away from pissing on it. Still, there are 25 cars to be won! Mind you, if I won, I'd probably give 23 of them away. And all for £1.10.

New Year's Daze: A memorable new year for ITV as several regional channels went off air having lost their franchises due to a money-grabbing bidding war the previous year. More on that shortly. Elsewhere, more Clive James on BBC One, Rab C Nesbitt on BBC Two and Channel 4 trusting its new hit series to see out the year with a live "Big Breakfast End of Year Show", a late but not especially naughty edition of its hugely successful new morning show.

Theme Nights: Another love letter to TV comes in the form of BBC Two's "Granadaland" tardily paying back Granada Television's "Tribute To The BBC" from 1956. Programmes include a documentary on the station, a look at music from the region, Colin Welland's 1970 comic play "Roll On Four O'clock" and a new "Pro-Celebrity" episode of "University Challenge" which had ended on ITV in 1987 and wouldn't reappear until 1994 on this very channel. Oh and an episode of some Mancunian soap opera or other. Sure it'll never catch on.

Wouldn't Happen Now: "Eldorado" on BBC One's Christmas Day schedule is definitely a unique one. As befitting the time of Baby Jesus doing a birth, there's a lot of religious programming. Looking with modern eyes, it reminds me how quickly TV scraped down its commitment to "the God slot" as the 90s progressed. At the time I was delighted but looking at what they're putting out on Sunday teatimes instead, maybe a bit of Harry Secombe's ghost bellowing up a monastery is what the World needs right now.

New For '93: Despite the new regional channels it's a sparse January for new series with downbeat but extremely popular series "Watching" and Jimmy Nail's "Spender" back back BACK! New laughs came from the painfully honest break-up comedy "Joking Apart" by Steven Moffat, Jasper Carrott's "The Detectives" and "Breakfast With Frost". Also on BBC One Marti Caine hosted the even shorter-lived "Your Best Shot" which is pretty much "You Bet!" but with the clever added twist of not being on ITV.

Is The Sound Of Music On? Yep, but you'll need Sky Movies Gold to see it I'm afraid.

Saturday, 19th December, 1992

9.25am: What's Up Doc? (ITV)

"This week's guests include Darren Day and actor John Altman, who plays Nick Cotton in EastEnders."

We've all been privy to some stupid pub or playground conversations in our lives. Religion. Politics. Football. And I can manage to stay out of all of them. But start a conversation on the best Saturday morning TV show of all time and I'm in there boots first to discuss the subtleties of "Going Live" vs. "Get Fresh", the increase on our screens of Creamy Muck Muck in the noughties or why "Parallel 9" was a load of old toss. When asked for my favourite though, I always get blank looks followed invariably by the question "What the buggering arse was What's Up Doc?" Well, I'm glad you asked.

Broadcast for three series between 1992 and 1995, "What's Up Doc?" was a replacement for the long-running but fairly dull magazine show "Motormouth" which copied its BBC rival "Going Live!" massively but with the added twist of being less good. If anything was going to beat imperial phase Schofield and Greene it would need to go so completely the other way that kids would love it, parents would be reminded of "TISWAS" and advertisers would wonder if the creators needed basic psychiatric help. That was "What's Up Doc?" a home to the usual cartoons, pop stars and competitions you'd expect from a Saturday mornings but also some of the most freakish, brilliant and appalling characters ever seen outside of a Troma film. This is a unique world of puppets, costumed lunatics and humans having the absolute time of their lives, a fact confirmed in the series' first Christmas show by co-presenter Andy Crane creasing himself laughing off screen throughout the opening minutes. He is joined by his fellow hosts Pat Sharp and Yvette Fielding who have decided to all be "lovely and nice" because it's Christmas and to help them with proceedings are their resident human-sized hybrid French stereotype frog man Gaston[18] who is giving mulled wine to all the children, the cheese obsessed Simon Perry[19], a 3000-year-old woman named Cassie[20], irritating furball Baljit...and who's hiding inside the polystyrene snowman? *"Oh my eyes are bulging out, its nasty Nick Cotton!"*, cries Yvette as the soap actor turns up to menace the kids at the same time as promoting his panto in Maidstone where this episode just happened to go out from.

"The stars of the new Muppet movie hope to pay a surprise visit to What's Up Doc?" (Radio Times capsule description)

Not much of a surprise if it's in the Radio Times, is it? Also it's Andy Crane who goes to them at London's Trocadero for a fun interview with Kermit, Miss Piggy and Gonzo plus the director Brian Henson about "The Muppet Christmas Carol" which had been released in cinemas the previous day. Now the film has long been taken to heart as a seasonal classic it is bizarre but beautiful

---

[18] Saturday morning staple Peter Cocks in heavy makeup. He would later change during the episode to play Simon Perry's equally geeky friend Colin.

[19] Stephen Taylor Woodrow playing a character later repackaged in the later as "Norm" from the Twix adverts

[20] Controlled and voiced by Steve Nallon, possibly best known for his work as the voice of Thatcher on "Spitting Image".

to see it as a contemporary release even if it'd be a whole five years before it saw a terrestrial airing with ITV showing it on Christmas Day 1997.

Of course there still needs to be boring bits to remind people it's still a children's programme and that's covered by the awful Darren Day promoting the long blotted out "Teen Win Lose or Draw" and chefs Greg and Max making a Christmas cake on location for a nonplussed grandma. There's also music from the appalling New Jack Swing tedium of Louie Louie and Boney M…or rather the one surviving member and some others (*"more like Barely M"* said my friend on re-watching) performing a medley of their hits. At least the cartoons - "Batman The Animated Series" and "Taz-Mania" - are both brand spanking new and brilliant thanks to Warner Bros who backed the series with TVS[21]. The episode closes with a pre-filmed Christmas dinner sketch featuring all the characters and occasional guest star Frank Sidebottom becoming increasingly manic, food-splattered and involves at least one character being boiled alive. The man inside the big head Chris Sievey had been contributing one of the series' most memorable features - the soap parody "Life With The Amoebas" (no one can see them 'cos they're small...very very small...) - about an almost invisible one-cell family represented on screen by giant arrows. This was always my favourite part of the show as a kid and it came as a pleasant but oddly unexpected surprise when I found out who was behind it decades later.

[21] Before TVS lost its licence and Scottish TV took over.

The jokes are often filthy and a jumbo jet height above the kids' heads (*"That halo is crooked",* Simon says to nativity Virgin Mary Cassie who sighs *"One little slip up in the blackout and a woman's reputation is tarnished forever!"*), inappropriate (John Altman reading "Serial Killer Magazine" as the show's resident child eating wolves Bro and Bro run around with a chainsaw) or legitimately surreal (a worm argues with a Geordie sock and a human sized box man screams "HAVE YEW GOT A LOIGHT BOYYYYYY") If this sounds all a bit too unhinged to continue you'd be onto something as almost all of above were jettisoned for the anaemic third and final run after several complaints to the ITC over the content leading to show creators Vanessa Hill and Ged Allen walking off the show midway through series two rather than water it down. People who have seen the beef waistcoat-wearing Mr Spanky with his the ghee-spraying 'Naughty Torty' will not forget in a hurry.

Its light burned quickly but for a generation of warped little idiots like me "What's Up Doc?" was hilarious, inventive, stupid, unsettling, brilliant, exhilarating, mad, jaw-dropping and, for a time, everything.

Sunday, 20th December, 1992

7.45pm: So Haunt Me (BBC One)

"Yetta meets her new grandson, and it's the happiest day of her death."

A curio from the short-lived period when BBC One was in the business of commissioning high-concept sitcoms: Karl Howman as an apprentice Grim Reaper? Check. Nicholas Lyndhurst flitting between two decades through a time portal[22]? Sure, why not! Miriam Karlin as an elderly Jewish ghost who stays in the house she died in despite a new young family living there? Um...

Beginning in February 1992, the first series had been enough of a success for an almost instant repeat run to follow with this Christmas special heralding the start of the second set of episodes. However, if you'd had the poor grace to miss any of those airings, you might not be in luck here as the episode cracks on apace assuming you're entirely on board with the events of the first series. Supposing you are one of those unlucky people, a running thread throughout had been Yetta's desire to reconnect with her daughter Carole ("Carole with an E" was the series' one major catchphrase) which she finally does in this Christmas special. She also isn't visible to everyone but then sometimes is. Yeah. Other than that it's fairly standard sitcom trope central - precocious children, over-sharing neighbours, a stroppy teenager becoming vegetarian on Christmas Day, over-bearing mothers and child-like Dads impatient for their presents. As for the Jewish gags, they're a nice change of pace for a prime-time sitcom but they're obviously somewhat of their era. It's not a bad half hour of comedy - an "Exorcist" sight gag is particularly nicely played - with a great cast including George Costigan and Tessa Peake-Jones.

Keeping with the high concepts, creator Paul Mendelson would go onto produce "My Hero" (2000-06), a superhero themed sitcom that can best be described as "on once".

---

[22] Mulberry (1992-93) and "Goodnight Sweetheart" (1993-99)

Monday, 21st December, 1992

4.25pm: Rhino Christmas (Channel 4)

"Mott wishes it would snow this Christmas. Then a rhino from her dreams turns up and somehow the prospect looks stronger."

A charming short film from Screen Australia featuring a bored young girl looking for something to perk up Christmas Day in the suburbs. At the same time two equally fed up council workers take their bulldozer on the road in search of real coffee. Astoundingly these two threads do dovetail wonderfully with the help of a strange talking puppet rhinoceros. *"Twas the night before Christmas, when all through the house / not a creature was stirring....not even a rhinocer-ouse..."*

It's an interesting look at how Christmas Day really was (I mean, this was 30 years ago but I suspect much of it still applies) for a country we see on telly all the time yet know surprisingly little about culturally outside Paul Hogan, Bouncer the dog and Blinky Bill pissed up on Castlemaine XXXX. A fantasy at heart, it also captures that frustration and excitement you feel as a kid when the grown-ups are dead to the world in bed and the world belongs to you. It's really funny and hugely individual, with an accordion playing Polish man, scat singing kids swapping their crap presents, clock radios with big moving mouths, broadcasts on the microwave, new age parents, a dog called Batman, a huge homemade snow making machine and an ending which borders on the legitimately eerie. Strange video game graphics and wobbly video effects enhance the dream sequences and flashbacks giving it a unique look from the usual Aussie fare kids were used to such as "Pugwall" or "Round The Twist" although it definitely wouldn't be out of place as a story on the latter.

No future pop stars here sadly but older viewers might recognise the late Lynda Gibson who appeared as Matron Dorothy Conniving-Bitch in the spoof soap opera "Let the Blood Run Free" from Channel 4 in the early 90s. Behind both the script and camera was John Armstrong, one of the leading lights in children's programming with recent credits on "H20: Just Add Water"[23], "Dennis and Gnasher", CBBC staple "The Deep" and even the legendary "Bananas in Pyjamas". With a career of over thirty years in kids TV, it's no surprise that this is a lovely half hour scheduled by Channel 4 in a slot now more associated by awful people buying tasteless properties or insulting each other's food. Perhaps we all need a little rhino magic of our own…

Tuesday, 22 December, 1992

8.00pm: 2 Point 4 Children (BBC One)

"A Christmas edition of the comedy by Andrew Marshall, starring Belinda Lang and Gary Olsen"

The first of six seasonally scheduled specials from a terrific sitcom that was never quite big enough to make it onto the Christmas Day schedule yet remained a constant favourite throughout the nineties. Ostensibly a straight forward family sitcom with a frustrated mum, childish dad, horror-obsessed son and stroppy

---

[23] That teen mermaid drama you keep seeing pop up on Netflix. I refuse to believe that you haven't.

teenage daughter, the Porter family lived in a world where the strange can and frequently does happen. So with a touch of the bizarre already bedded into the sitcom's DNA, the Christmas special is where "2 Point 4 Children" really had some fun and the first of these – "Misery" – appeared between the second and third series. Bill (Belinda Lang) and Ben (Gary Olsen) are looking over hotel brochures to save spending the holiday with the former's overbearing and guilt-tripping mother Bette (played by a suitably horrible Liz Smith) knowing full well the inevitable will occur. The most 'regular' story-wise but still packed with laughs though jokes about programming the video, Bruno Brookes on the radio and "not getting your fonts to bitmap" date it slightly. Unlike the usual series, dream sequences feature including a brilliant parody of the Stephen King film it shares an episode title with, perpetually randy neighbour Rona imagining a very naughty Santa and a closing tribute to "Bing Como". These all singing, all dancing finales would become a staple of the seasonal shows with Gary Olsen getting to indulge some old fashioned slapstick.

The weirdness really begins with 1993's "Babes in the Wood" when the family finally get to do the hotel holiday plan only to get lost in the middle of a very foggy nowhere and, in true horror form, start to disappear one by one. This is where Andrew Marshall really shines, having honed his gruesomeness with his writing partner David Renwick on the likes of "Whoops Apocalypse" and spoof horror anthology "The Steam Video Company". While everything is ultimately alright because it's a pre-watershed BBC sitcom, Marshall doesn't undersell the scary scenes with a creepy abandoned house and violent prisoner on the run thrown in the mix for good measure…

A promotion to Boxing Day came with 1994's "Relax-ay-Voo" where once again there's an argument about where to spend the holiday – Ben wants to sneak off to France through the newly opened Channel Tunnel, Bill just wants to hide at home. Starting with a particularly good bit of silent comedy with Ben and son David (John Pickard) getting ever bigger and bigger Christmas trees before a truly of its time conversation about the dangers of connecting to the internet via which some mysterious messages begin to appear offering some unusual Christmas wishes with a hint of "WarGames". Unless… there's not another Bill they could be thinking of…?

Christmas Eve was home to the 1995 special "Porky's" which is brilliantly summed up by the Radio Times blurb *"In a display of poor judgment, Bill entrusts Ben with buying all the food for Christmas."* In this case: a very large live pig which the latter had won in a tombola and neglected to inform the rest of the family about for months on end. The episode revolves around their attempts to get rid of it and…well, that's about it. But by this point the cast were so comfortable in their characters that Marshall it's still hugely entertaining just watching them interact with each other. 1996's "Two Years before the Mast" is another high concept one and for once the cast actually get off the studio set as a series of accidents lead to the family (including Ben's annoying sister Tina, played by Sandra Dickinson) ending up as stowaways on a cruise. It's the weakest of the bunch but that could be due to Marshall's workload with one of his sitcoms (the medical comedy "Health and Efficiency") just ended and another ("Dad" starring George Cole and Kevin McNally) launching in 1997. It could also be the reason why no more proper Christmas specials appeared in 1997 or 1998.

Which just leaves us with "The Millennium Experience" from the 30th December 1999[24], the final episode of series eight and, for a number of reasons, the final episode of the whole run. By now eldest child Jenny (Claire Buckfield) was at University, David was grown out of his creepy obsessions and the family had adopted a pre-teen named Declan (Alex Kew). The episode really captures the panic, enthusiasm and uncertainty about the end of the century yet rings ominously current as I write this with Ben panic buying toilet rolls, electric generators and water tanks due to media scare-mongering. Bill insists on getting rid of them all and thus, in true sitcom style, the family ultimately see the New Year without gas, water and electric keeping sane by sharing secrets and their reminiscences of some of the series' more memorable moments.

Despite the frequent oddness they could endure, these were characters that felt real in a way that sitcom families so often don't with a household really struggling through the early 90s recession and kids that actually are allowed to age up and develop as the series progresses. It's a series that could've continued on and off for years but the horrible early death of the irreplaceable Gary Olsen on the 12th September 2000 aged just 42 would bring a close to the weird world of the Porters. It was a double blow not just for the loss of a great comic actor but a character that felt tangible and lovable thanks to a wonderful cast and tremendous, human writing that adapted to whatever times it was going through. Especially at Christmas…

[24] Just after the similarly themed "Dinnerladies" episode "Minnellium".

Thursday, 24th December, 1992

5.10pm: Happy Days Reunion Special (Channel 4)

"Henry Winkler hosts a nostalgic look back at the American comedy series."

"Happy Days" always confused me as a child. It was on constantly in the 1980s yet was set in the 1950s but apparently it was made in the 1970s?! . There was even a 1980 Hanna-Barbera cartoon spin-off – "The Fonz and The Happy Days Gang"- where Doctor Wh…sorry, Fonzie uses a time machine brought by Cupcake, a girl from the future with a dog named Mr Cool. Because cartoons. Despite ITV being the first to show it in the UK from 1976 it always seemed a better fit for the import-heavy Channel 4 who would cycle through the complete run many times over the next two decades. This April 1992 reunion for ABC in the US didn't seem to be for anything in particular and had no real excitement to it as the old episodes were still being regularly shown all over the world. They got Ron Howard at least, along with Tom Bosley, Marion Ross and Scott Baio before he went insane. A further reunion occurred in 2005 although any planned future ones might be a bit awkward thanks to a $10 million lawsuit brought in 2011 by several cast members including Erin Moran, Donnie Most, Marion Ross and Anson Williams who learned they weren't getting any money from their youthful faces being slapped on a myriad of new retro-themed items including a themed casino slot machine none of them had been informed of. The cast only learned it was a thing when a friend of the former Mrs C saw it in the wild and found that "players win the jackpot when five Marion Rosses are rolled." Each actor ultimately received a payment of $65,000. Happy Days indeed.

Friday, 25th December, 1992

8.10am: Edd the Duck's Megastar Treck (BBC One)

"A galaxy of stars join Quacktain Berk on the starship Intrepedd."

For those who were lucky enough to be too young or too drunk between 1988 and 1993, Edd The Duck was a "funky" green haired puppet that could only communicate in quacks – aka producer Christina Mackay-Robinson under a table using a duck whistle - with whichever presenter was hosting Children's BBC in the 'Broom Cupboard'. After being slow to react to merchandising his puppet precursor Gordon T Gopher they went the other way here with toys, plushes, books, videos. bubble bath, stationary, clothing, puzzles, those things you stick in your car window like Garfield, two indisputably appalling video games and even a 1990 single "Awesome Dood!" which shockingly did not trouble the top 40.

An acquired taste, he could certainly pull in the stars with this "Star Trek" parody containing Lesley Joseph, Des Lynam, Anne Diamond, Nick Owen, Anthea Turner, the Minogue sisters and...Punt and Dennis??? Still appearing as part of the very not for kids "Mary Whitehouse Experience", the duo play aliens beaming up TV celebrities with the latter pretty much doing his Mr Strange character. You know..."Milky Milky" and all that. An end credit line reads "Martian material by Steve Punt and Hugh Dennis" which much surely had been a first for television. It's a ten minute bit of fluff made for kids up far too early on Christmas morning and yet it drains me so with its terribleness. Andi Peters plays "Mr Sock" and – ho ho - Scotty is an actual Scottie dog. Philippa

Forrester in a scandalously short dress definitely falls into the "something for the dads" category although if they've any sense they'll all still be fast asleep.

Saturday, 26th December, 1992

6.50pm: Noel's Christmas House Party (BBC One)

"Leading lights from the Amateur Dramatic Society turn up to rehearse Cinderella with a difference..."

Success is a bitch queen from a far and distant planet. The person who rules the media one minute could be selling newspapers the next and no more so than the cut throat world of very light entertainment. In the modern age there's a bit of a void when it comes to competent presenters who can handle the big razzle dazzle of a variety show, switching from game show grins to sob story pouts in one move. And those that do exist learned it all from Noel Edmonds.

Never afraid to stick his tidy beard out wherever an opportunity presented, Noel began on the wireless and quickly rose up the ranks becoming, aged just 24, the second host of the prestigious Radio 1 breakfast show after Tony Blackburn. More on him in a minute. Eventually "Top of the Pops" called and Edmonds became a regular host leading to more TV work including a kids' call-in series called "Z-Shed" which was expanded into a Saturday morning magazine series entitled the "Multi-Coloured Swap Shop". Here, he became an icon to millions of kids but struggled to find that vehicle that would transfer him to proper big people's telly with "Hobby Horses", "Noel Edmonds' Lucky Numbers" and a revival of "Juke Box Jury" quickly coming and going. This would be the bit in the biopic where Noel would look sad for a bit then get a brilliant idea of taking all the best bits from "Swap Shop" - phone in competitions, pop bands, daft clips and celebrity guests - and putting it out live on a Saturday night.

And so in September 1982 "The Late, Late Breakfast Show" came to be and, after a wobbly start, would develop into an enormous success over four years with many of Noel's trademark bits like hidden camera surprises, bantering with the audience and big stunts originating there. Sadly anyone of a certain age will tell you the one thing it's actually memorable for: the 1986 death of Michael Lush, a member of the public who was the unfortunate victim of a bungee cord accident when rehearsing for one of those big stunts. The series was pulled bar his now traditional Christmas morning live broadcasts and would soon transform into the sentimental "Noel's Christmas Presents" in which the bearded one made deserved people's wishes come true.

After the dust had settled Noel returned to Saturday nights in 1988 with his "Saturday Roadshow", a quite fun premise that always insisted it was being broadcast from a remote location despite clearly being a BBC studio set. Features-wise, it was much the same as his earlier live show and, penance met, lead to his biggest success of them all - "Noel's House Party".

Starting in September 1991, this was Noel in his element as the supposed owner of a stately pile called Crinkley Bottom that was always being invaded by famous folk on a Saturday night. As we join him for this live episode midway through the second series, the "House Party" is in its grandest era, helped but not yet ruined by a certain pink spotty creature that would come to dominate the following year. Mr Blobby had originally been designed as a fake kids TV character to prank unsuspecting celebrities in the "Gotcha" section before becoming a genuine kids TV favourite. As if to nod at his future ubiquity, Blobby is part of a sketch where he manages to appear on "This Morning", "Grandstand", "Film '92", "Casualty", "The Late Show" and "Top of the Pops", a year before his self-titled track would hit the top spot on that very programme.

Speaking of annoying jerks from the past, CBBC's Andi Peters is back with a bearded Edd The Duck who wishes to be known as "Noel Eddmonds" but there's no time for them as the programme is constantly running from one feature to another. It's hard not to join in the excitement as Noel breathlessly rushes through features like "Wait Till I Get You Home", "Grab A Grand" and the still hugely exciting and different hidden live camera segment "NTV" although an anecdote by the 'victim' about putting the wrong false teeth in a corpse is a bit extreme for tea-time telly. Perhaps because it's a live show on Boxing night the celebrity guests are an odd bunch with Joe Longthorne holding a perplexed dog during his frankly exhausting act, Pat Coombs as a dotty organist, some blokes off "The Bill" knocking on the door and Frank Thornton popping up for a daft gag right at the end. Frank Bruno and Nigel Benn are also in the house as part of a public phone vote in for which of them deserves a good gunging (with over seventy thousand people ringing in to slime Bruno.) And then there's Tony Blackburn, that episode's "Gotcha" recipient, who is taken in by a fake pink-smock wearing, nettle soup eating "religious group" He's a great sport and comes across sincere and charming as people learned when he became King of the Jungle a decade later. Comedy fans will also be pleased that one of the actors in the scene is a young Rebecca Front.

A genuine unexpected treat - and I don't mean Noel's garish waistcoat - "Noel's House Party" was a mix of sketch show, game show, children's programme and hidden camera series that shouldn't have hung together and yet did for nearly a decade, coming to an end under a bit of a cloud in 1999. Noel would be slung back into the wilderness, going a bit bonkers in the process, before a quiz show about opening random boxes would put him back in the spotlight again five years later. Merry Blobmas!

Wednesday, 30th December, 1992

10.30pm: Nightingales (Channel 4)

"Return of the black comedy series written by Paul Makin, about three unorthodox security guards."

You know those shows that you're fairly sure only you saw and seemed impossible to track down in the pre-Wikipedia age? Those comedy programmes late night that you laughed at but were never entirely sure what you were laughing at? The TV made for the smallest group of people - all of whom treasure it to this day? That was "Nightingales", a series surreal in its very DNA. Take this episode "Silent Night": the luckless night watchmen are working over Christmas Eve when they are greeted by a young lady called Mary (Lia Williams) who just happens to be pregnant and about to give birth. Being smart to sitcom tropes, the frustrated cod-philosopher of the bunch Carter (Robert Lindsay) makes her promise she's not an allegory. Meanwhile the token idiot of the group "Ding Dong" Bell (David Threlfall) has bought his kids Easter eggs for Christmas as they're cheap in the shops and the optimistic older member of the group Sarge (James Ellis) is trying to keep morale up despite nobody (*"Harold Pinter, The Pope..."*) they invited to their Christmas carol service turning up. Despite the irregularity and literary pretensions, it's a fast-paced and incredibly funny half hour that deserves to be as well-known as "A Christmassy Ted" or any of its contemporaries with "The Young Ones" probably its closest comparison in terms of tone.

This was the start of the second and final run which would carry on until February 1993 although viewers wouldn't be blamed for forgetting series one had happened considering it had aired nearly three years earlier in February 1990, leaving many assuming it had simply long been cancelled. The problem with having a prestige cast like this one is that they end up being a bit busy with even the director Tony Dow fitting it in around episodes of "Only Fools and Horses". This only underlines how much it was clearly a passion project for all involved.

There was a haunting mysteriousness to the episodes all set in the small hours of the night where nothing nasty really much happened (the DVD release is a PG) but lots of oddness is suggested and the series finale still unsettles me to this day. The series' sole writer Paul Makin would go on to write for "Goodnight Sweetheart" and the forgotten "Grown Ups" before dying aged just 54 in 2008. This series is a hell of a legacy though and one which will bewitch newcomers for decades to come. *"Christmas? What a load of old wank."*

Wednesday, 30th December, 1992

5.10am: America's Top Ten (ITV)

"The top ten albums of 1992. Presented by Richard Blade."

Richard Who[25]? Where's Casey Kasem?

Depending on which ITV region you lived in, the syndicated American pop show "America's Top Ten" was a regular sight around the schedules, either cropping up after "The Chart Show" on Saturday lunchtimes or in the middle of the night as post-pub filler. Hosted by one of the US' most popular DJs slash Shaggys from "Scooby Doo", Casey Kasem this was a slick rundown of what was going on in pop from 1980 until the year it came to an end…1992. So what was in the rundown of the biggest albums of 1992? "Copper Blue" by Sugar? Therapy's debut "Nurse"? Perhaps "XYZ" by Moose? No of course not. The previous year's "Nevermind" and "Metallica" LPs are in there as is U2's November 1991 release "Achtung Baby" but so are TWO releases by Garth Brooks next to Billy Ray Cyrus and a pre-self-aware Michael Bolton. Only "Totally Krossed Out" by Kris Kross feels like something approaching the actual spirit of the year just passed[26].

---

[25] Amazingly not his real name. Richard Blade is actually from Bristol and christened Richard Sheppard in 1952 taking his nickname from "Blade Runner". He apparently remains a huge deal in LA radio.

[26] My source for this is the Billboard 200 Year End albums by the way; a confusing mess of nonsense that may not even have been used on the series.

Thursday, 31st December, 1992

10.45pm: The End of the Year Show (ITV)

"Highlights from 25 years of light entertainment and drama from Thames."

The television equivalent of an ex reminding you what you were letting go as Thames counted down its final 75 minutes on air before Carlton Television took over the licence for London's weekday part of the ITV network. For those under a certain age, the idea of ITV being divided up into small sections might seem a bit strange outside of the localised news reports at 6pm but much local pride would be taken in the local telly franchise with TV presenters often saying people were from "Granadaland" (the North West) or "ATV-land" (the Midlands, later taken over by Central.) You'd come to know all the station idents before the programmes from London Weekend Television's line-drawing bombast, the bleepy synths of Tyne Tees, the wobbly and dream-like HTV and of course Thames reflecting itself in the water.

The children's magazine "Look-In" (1971-94) would publish the telly highlights for all fourteen regions and I would be captivated by the differences between them. "Oh look, Anglia and LWT are showing "Blockbusters" but HTV and Central have "Cartoon Alphabet"..." At which point I'd try and imagine what these other programmes were like and cursing those lucky swines near a border who could twiddle their aerial to their neighbouring county! No such luck for me in the Yorkshire TV area as I felt I may never learn what a Gus Honeybun magic birthday would be like! Or what exactly WAS a "Puffin's Pla(i)ce"?

The companies who ran the TV franchises had to keep to guidelines which would be tracked initially by the ITA (Independent Television Authority) becoming the Independent Broadcasting Authority in 1972 so as to cover radio too. I'm simplifying the whole thing for space but this was basically to ensure viewers got a good mix of quality programming rather than just razzle dazzle and cheese. A few franchisees came and went in 1982 but things remained on a largely even keel until Thatcher's government pushed through the Broadcasting Act of 1990 which would remove many of the previous guidelines as a push towards deregulation. The IBA was abolished and replaced with the less strict ITC. Suddenly it became about how much money you had to bid for your channel, not quality of programming promised. This for many is when television as it used to be died for good. Some counties kept their franchise due to lack of opposition whilst others had to pay through the nose to hang on. Some were confident their long standing would see them through and were shattered to learn otherwise - TVS losing to Meridian, TSW to Westcountry, TV-am to GMTV and perhaps the biggest shock of all, Thames Television being outbid by £10 million from the deep pockets of Carlton Television who would use this as a base to expand into other ITV stations creating the amorphous blob that is the current ITV plc.

And so Thames were right to feel a bit cheesed off as they said their final goodbyes reminding everyone of the programmes they'd made since 1968 including "The Naked Civil Servant", "The Sooty Show", "Rumpole of the Bailey", "Wish You Were Here...?", "The Wind In The Willows", "The Kenny Everett Video Show", "Mr Bean" and "Minder", followed by a final goodbye from Richard

Dunn, the channel's Chief Executive and a final montage backed by The Tourists' cover of "I Only Want To Be With You". And then it was all over. ITN were next to see in the New Year bongs before Chris Tarrant appeared in Trafalgar Square to see in the new station. Did he know everything was about to change about commercial TV? And was that his final answer? Only time would tell…

Friday. 1st January, 1993

10.00pm: Rory Bremner ...and the Morning After the Year Before (Channel 4)

"John Major wakes up on New Year's Day with no memory of the events of 1992. Luckily, he has recorded the previous night's Rory Bremner Show, and it all comes flooding back."

A special kicking off Rory Bremner's seventeen years at Channel 4 after seven series at the BBC and countless appearances on everything from Radio 4's satirical revue "WeekEnding" to the Jimmy Cricket's ITV sketch show "And There's More". The last of these BBC shows was barely six months old when he was popped up here with a satirical look back at the previous year. A hugely talented impersonator who'd broken through in his early twenties, Bremner had slowly added a more political side to his work as he'd gone on even if he wasn't quite ready to let go of the likes of Roger Moore, Denis Norden, Michael Fish, Geoff Boycott, Harry Carpenter, Barry Norman and Ronnie Corbett just yet, preferring to weave them into a more topical script with Bob

Monkhouse here asking which MPs have actually read the Maastricht Treaty.

Beginning with cricket, Radio 4 and "The Prisoner" jokes in the first two minutes; this is a programme setting out its stall as a show for the more discerning, perhaps older viewer. The framing device of a cloudy John Major watching the programme himself is a smart one as is the fake continuity announcement *"some more smart-arsed satire from the bloke we pinched from the BBC".* Ultimately, it's just more of what Bremner became known for and giving a flavour of the era of which it was recorded are jokes about Benetton, Sinead O'Connor ripping up a photo of the Pope, Labour being eternal losers, Paddy Ashdown being a shagger, "Gladiators", the Queen in a smoking Windsor Castle, "don't you just love being in control?", Nigel Mansell being boring, the moving of Women's Hour to the morning, "Michael Winner's True Crimes", David Mellor also being a shagger, Right Said Fred, Sky stealing the football coverage, Bill Clinton "not inhaling", Madonna's "Sex" book, Woody Allen doing...oh you know and aforementioned Carlton TV takeover.

Bremner seems much older than his 31 years at the time this was made and as someone who lived through that year it still holds up, bar some brownface for a Trevor McDonald impersonation which feels a real misstep. Not a lot of unusual impressions in there but a short segment with Rory as fellow Channel 4 celebrities Tony Slattery, Clive Anderson and Paul Merton is great fun as is his thuggish Ken Clarke. Sadly, despite them being part of his later BBC series, John Bird and John Fortune are not featured here but would soon reappear later that year in "Rory Bremner, Who

Else?" and the more egalitarian follow up series "Bremner, Bird and Fortune".

Ultimately it's an interesting nostalgia trip, not exactly railing at any single party or getting angry in any way, merely pointing out the mistakes that were made along the way. In the current climate, it makes me unsurprisingly nostalgic for a time where misbehaving MPs apologised or even stepped down.

1993

Highest Rated Programme: The BBC once again cleaned up with the Trotters topping the bill for the 25th and Boxing Day's "One Foot In The Algarve" doing the best business of the whole week with 20 million viewers enjoying the 'Meldrews abroad' special.

Big Films on the BBC: BBC One start Christmas week with the exciting new Sean Connery game show "The Hunt For Red October" before Christmas Day brought the odd partnership of "Back To The Future Part III" and "Ghost" with the latter managing to freak out over 18 million viewers thanks to that bit with the falling glass pane at the end. Those who complained about a lack of cubes being gleamed the previous Christmas will be delighted to know BBC Two has Christian Slater's skateboard thriller "Gleaming The Cube" for the youth. There's also room for the original yet still terrifying "family" fantasy "The Witches", Michael Palin's "American Friends" and the 1989 Woody Allen thriller "Crimes and Misdemeanours" which premiered on Two at the exact same time Channel 4 showed his classic "Manhattan".

Big Films on ITV: The 25th had movies all the way with "National Lampoon's Christmas Vacation" at 6pm followed by fantasy drama "Field of Dreams" and wobbly thriller "DOA". But don't worry, there's still room for "Police Academy 6: City Under Siege" on December 27th. Bond was also back in "The Man with the Golden Gun" that same day but viewers would have to wait until 3rd January 1994 for the terrestrial premiere of "Licence to Kill".

Big Films on Channel 4: Lots of obscurities as part of a "Christmas In New York" theme week leading up to the first showing of 1989's "New York Stories", a strange and not entirely successful triptych of shorts by Martin Scorsese, Francis Ford Coppola and that Woody Allen again. Late Christmas night "Monkey Business" launched another Marx Brothers season.

Oh That Queen's Speech: A pretty heavy one with talk of conflict in the Middle East and Northern Ireland and the 75th anniversary of the First World War. She also mentioned the "Global Village" we now lived in and the concern we'd soon be dominated by constant overwhelming news. With Diana's death leading to 24 hour news cycles and constant online updates its hard not to agree, y'Majesty.

For The Kids: Zoe Ball and Chris Jarvis look on as another repeated drama serial props up a sparse pre-Christmas week on BBC One with the New Zealand sci-fi production "The Night of the Red Hunter", "Defenders of the Earth" and "Playdays". On ITV "The New Adventures of He-Man" has been joined by 'futuristic animation' "COPS" which was so far ahead its time it had been out of production for nearly five years. At least Channel 4 now have boots in the game with an eccentric line-up containing repeats of "The Lone Ranger", Rik Mayall's "Grim Tales", French nothing "Spiff and Hercules", "Saved by the Bell" and whatever "Sharky and George" was meant to be. And yes, I still know all the words to the theme tune…

The Pops: It's the last stand for Dortie and Franklin as common sense prevailed and "Top of the Pops" got back to basics in 1994. But have they got a big year to go out on? Um, no…outside a double-dipping Take That and the idea of elderly relatives seeing "Informer" by Snow for the first time (even if Dortie introducing it saying "*Reggae finally got the exposure it deserved*" was probably ill-advised…) it's a bloody boring line-up thanks to Gabrielle, The Bluebells (in kilts and clasping a stuffed Scottie dog because… Scotland?), Ace of Base and M People making it into the studio. Elsewhere 2 Unlimited performed "No Limits" with a backing set of dancers more suited for laser tag plus far too much Michael Jackson for the holy day. And Mr Blobby didn't even perform his Christmas No.1 live! Also: as it's a Saturday, "The Chart Show" is on ITV at half 11 though there'll be sadly no awkward sepia photographs of an indie band today as it's the dance chart.

Radio Times Cover: Another outdoor snow scene as a gap-toothed Jonny Briggs lookalike in full Santa outfit lets his beard slip while he stares gormlessly into space. Sales down to 3.7 million but we're up to "over 700 films!" £1.30.

TV Times Cover: There's something just very "TV Times" about the zany illustration of a Santa with his elves riding a jalopy through a snow scene. Far too common for "Radio Times" but not featuring a soap star's face enough for the cheaper listings mags. In other news, there's only £125,000 to be won! And details of over 800 films! I'm not sure where the extra one hundred movies came from, mind. A snip at £1.25.

New Year's Daze: BBC Two greeted the New Year for the first time with "Jools Holland's Hootenanny" featuring Sting, the Gipsy Kings and Sly and Robbie. The programme, originally spun off from The Late Show - hence the Later tag - would steadfastly stick to its midnight slot for several years before becoming the 11pm-ish slot behemoth in 2002, where it remains to this day. Clive James continues running down the year on BBC One and ITV once again fail to bother sticking out an evening of films with "Bonnie and Clyde" taking us into the new year. Channel 4 returned to their concept of sticking cameras in different countries as the "New Year's Eve Triple Whammy" followed midnight around the world beginning with Cape Town at 10pm then Prague at 11pm and Dublin at 12pm.

Theme Nights: Two absolute belters from BBC Two. First up on December 18th was "Arena: Radio Night" an evening of shows about and featuring the wireless that featured interactions between the cigar-smoking, beer drinking "Television" (voiced by Peter Cook hidden behind a testcard) and the more refined "Radio" (the voice of Josie Lawrence) who could only be heard by playing Radio 4 at the same time as the TV broadcast. Highlights including the first ever televisual Shipping Forecast, a piece about London pirate stations and "TV Theft, Radio Rip Off" which explored the frequency radio shows were heading to telly at the time, including an early appearance by Alan Partridge and his producer Armando Iannucci.

December 27th saw us "At Home with Vic and Bob" with the new BBC signings given the whole channel to programme with archive telly and new sketches. The former consisted of a compilation of

Eric Idle's "Rutland Weekend Television", a rare 1972 "Dad's Army" sketch, documentary "Meerkats Utd" and Mike Leigh's brilliant "Nuts in May". The evening also offered the chance for viewers new and old to encounter the bra adorning Pat Arrowsmith and Dave Wright, troubled balladeers Mulligan and O'Hare and 1970s pop faves Slade in their family home. The most enduring item was a daft celebrity quiz knocked together with some of their friends called "Shooting Stars" which would go on to be quite popular over the next two decades. Channel 4 launched their first Christmas theme Week with the aforementioned "Christmas In New York" which begins worryingly enough with a short documentary about Trump Tower followed by the much more palatable "RuPaul's Christmas Ball".

Wouldn't Happen Now: No EastEnders in 1991 and now no Corrie in '93 as it's a Saturday!

New For '94: BBC One have the first series of Tim Firth's wonderful, underrated comic drama "All Quiet on the Preston Front" whilst Leslie Grantham-fronted undercover cop drama "99-1" and "Budgie The Little Helicopter" made their debuts on ITV. Over on Channel 4, the enduring "Time Team" was on route to getting its beard entangled around the schedules for the next decade. The winners were clearly BBC Two with "The All New Alexei Sayle Show", "The High Life", "Middlemarch" and "The Day Today" all launching that January. Those are the headlines… God I wish they weren't.

Is The Sound Of Music On? Sadly not.

Monday, 20th December, 1993

8.00pm: That's Showbusiness! (BBC One)

"The panel show that quizzes celebrities on their profession and confronts them with their past professional sins."

A quiz which seemed ever-present at one point, shifting from its initial good natured but dull tone in its early series with Gloria Hunniford and Kenny Everett as team captains to a more sarcastic "here's a photo of you looking slightly different!" yet still dull style by the end of its run in 1996. Mike Smith remained the host throughout and the Christmas Special from the 20th December 1993 is slap bang in the middle of this slightly arch shift as Michelle Collins and former "Casualty" actress Cathy Shipton tale on Nigel Havers and Keith Barron who had both recently appeared together in the already cancelled ITV comedy drama "The Good Guys". All are ribbed in some ways - there's an appearance in a very early TV role for Collins where she looks…much the same, a perfectly acceptable 60s pop ballad to embarrass Havers who played on it, a mortified-looking Shipton gamely plays along when asked to dance the Can Can and a thoroughly miserable Barron is asked to recite Dickie Valentine's "Christmas Alphabet". I ask you - is that showbusiness?!

Monday, 20th December, 1993

9.00pm: Newman and Baddiel Christmas in Pieces (BBC Two)

"David searches for a miracle and Robert goes North."

Making their name on the ground-breaking Radio 1 comedy series "The Mary Whitehouse Experience" before transferring it to TV with great success but less charm, 1993 found Rob Newman and David Baddiel ditching Punt and Dennis and playing up to their floppy haired indie-cred "comedy is the new rock n roll" personas. "In Pieces" dropped the 'gang show' feel of their early appearances in favour of both comedians performing their separate monologues from fake flat sets. Occasionally, the two would come together for sketches but they never look especially happy about it.

Baddiel is first up with comment that "God doesn't exist" although this is mainly the set up joke to how rubbish shower temperatures are. That's largely the tone of the full half hour which features a lot of references to old telly programmes or sex but not very much about Christmas. There are a few highlights including a short sketch about an unsubtle movie director, a Paul Daniels (Rob Newman wearing a bald wig tied on with very noticeable string) spoof with the Witchfinder General and, of course, "History Today", the breakthrough sketch from "The Mary Whitehouse Experience" involving the duo as old, respected professors talking to each other like children. The sight of an aged-up Newman shouting *"Look at me! I'm Eddie Kydd!"* as he tries to prove he doesn't need stabilisers before falling over a table truly made me laugh hard. Considering this well-established premise, it's odd that a second sketch featuring both as two young intellectuals on an arts series talking in high terms about having a fight (*"you are essentially moribund", "discourse, discourse, discourse"*) is exactly the same idea as the "History Today" sketches. Like much in this episode it feels like a bit of a off-cut as do a number of running bits that new viewers wouldn't have much chance of following. One such piece was the conclusion to Albert's (Denys Graham) story which got more unpleasant each week as the supposed "character actor" was forced to do increasingly nasty tasks for the pair in order to pay for his daughter's dialysis machine. The resolution, which I'll spare you the details of, shows a now wheelchair bound Albert happy, having finally paid for the medical equipment he needs before a moment that should be slapstick but ends up just vile and thoroughly disquieting. Elsewhere, Rob Newman's predatory Jarvis is still awful and has dated horrendously.

After the credits, the BBC's right to reply series "Bite Back" begins but, as that series aired on Sunday afternoons, it's a spoof featuring Albert dressed up to look like Newman who reads a statement inviting all of the audience to beat him up. Naturally, they do. The fact that Baddiel had already appeared on the real "Bite Back" the previous year to defend a, in hindsight, fairly indefensible line from "The Mary Whitehouse Experience" feels a bit 'cake and eating it'. A 25 date national tour followed culminating in a final date at Wembley Arena and that was it. Neither yet thirty, both went their separate ways and finding success on wildly different levels. It's doubly frustrating that "In Pieces" doesn't really work as there are genuine flashes of brilliance with some smart ideas and some annoyingly memorable catchphrases (*"Mr Bladyblub", "there was no need for that to happen", "as you do!"* and, of course, *"That's you that is"*) but it equally feels like the pair, who according to reports despised each other by this point, are more concerned with looking cool than being funny. Unquestionably popular with its target youth audience at the time it rarely seems to be thought of fondly – or at all - by many people today. Rest In Pieces.

Thursday, 23rd December, 1993

6.30pm: GamesMaster (Channel 4)

It's hard to express truly how necessary "GamesMaster" was. Video games had been featured on television since "Pong" first pinged in the 70s but coverage was either incredibly dry or cheerlessly mocked as something only for the kiddies despite the sales of the SNES, Mega Drive and Game Boy in particular going through the roof at the time the series' first aired.

Hosted from a real church and presented by relative newcomer Dominik Diamond the first series set the format that would stay pretty much unchanged from 1992 to 1998: three challenges on recently released games with "golden joysticks" for the winners - two for young contestants and one for a weekly celebrity guest - interspersed with reviews and children asking the "GamesMaster" for cheats and tips. This was a particularly inspired bit of casting with eccentric astrologer Patrick Moore in the title role under some neat screen graphics dishing out random cheat codes with bored distain bordering on anger. As the years progressed the sarcasm increased in Diamond's links with a barrage of barely-disguised innuendo. But he's gone for the episode I'm looking at here, unhappy with the announcement that McDonalds were sponsoring the third series which is where we find this special.

Taking over is an ill-prepared Dexter Fletcher, best known then as Spike in Steven Moffat's "Press Gang", dressed in a baby muck coloured jumpsuit and frequently bellowing for no reason. It's manic and loud and it only gets worse when he announces the guests for this 'all Panto Celebs' special as Aladdin (Woking), Dick

Whittington (Bath) and Dick Whittington (Croydon) go head-to-head. They couldn't even find a third different panto! And if you're thinking "I bet TV's 'Nasty Nick' is on again" you'd be bloody right as he chews a bit of scenery next to Lorraine Chase, Robin Askwith, Wayne Morris, Robert Duncan, Alf from Home and Away and some other people far too boring to talk about.

The first game played is an underwhelming Yogi Bear title in which the tiresome ursine has to collect clocks like what he always did in his many animated adventures. After some reviewers - including a very young Paul "Mr Biffo" Rose - pick their games of the year[27], similar challenges occur on "Alfred Chicken" and "Lemmings". The celebrity challenges were always my least favourite part with guests generally having no love or appreciation for video games and here a clueless Frank Bruno is handed his own bottom on a platter in little time by his daughter on the Mega Drive game "Greatest Heavyweights". Still, there's a chance to win the consoles of the future - a 3DO, a CDi, a CD32 and a Jaguar – all of which are presumably taking up valuable landfill space now. It's all very "yoof TV" – loud and bounding around when it didn't need to - patronising who they thought their audience was. Amazingly someone listened and the next series featured the return of Diamond as host before a short-sighted Channel 4 brought it to an end just as the next generation of consoles made gaming a much more accessible and profitable market.

Nothing really ever turned up to replace it directly but its tone and passion can be seen in hundreds of YouTube and Twitch channels

[27] FIFA, Zombies Ate My Neighbours, Sensible Soccer, Syndicate, Claymates and Street Fighter 2 Turbo.

today. Which is probably why E4 have commissioned a new version of the series for 2022!

Friday, 24th December, 1993

5.10pm: Maid Marian & Her Merry Men (BBC One)

"A handsome stranger comes to town."

By far one of the biggest hits Children's BBC had ever had, Tony Robinson's feminist reworking of the Robin Hood tale was a very funny sitcom for all the family with some incredibly catchy music and a dream cast including Kate Lonergan as the passionate Maid Marian, Wayne Morris as a yuppie fop version of Robin, Danny John-Jules as a rapping Rasta named Barrington and Robinson himself as the oily and devious Sheriff of Nottingham. Despite this episode appearing in the wake of the all-conquering "Robin Hood: Prince of Thieves" at the box office, "Maid Marian" had been a staple since November 1989 - just two weeks after Private Baldrick went over the top in "Blackadder Goes Forth".

Fads and faces were spoofed via the Merry Men and the dim inhabitants of the muddy town of Worksop including Red Nose Day, Fergie, "The Crystal Maze", Eurovision, Sonic, karaoke, "Masterchef", Michael Jackson, Aussie soaps and even The Beatles. "Maid Marian and Much the Mini-Mart Manager's Son" begins with everyone tap ..or perhaps mud dancing before the spectacularly dim Robin accidentally gives his identity away to the Sheriff...via personalised business cards with his full name and address. Lucky for him a colourful silver-tongued stranger appears and smooths things out. This is Much (Philip Wright) a dodgy Arthur Daley type character who can sell snow to a snowman quickly charming Marian into revealing out the Merry Men's secret forest hideout. Marian is a fully rounded figure that is both independent and spiky but also demanding and slow to trust so stripping her of what makes her so unique in the first place feels a bit out of character. Revenge is had however (*"He's a bloke...not a bowl of Coco Pops!"*) and a people's uprising against the supposed "Giant Toad Monster of Stoke-on-Trent" provides a big finish. The sets and costumes still look remarkable as do the "ex-Albanian army supplies" Much flogs everyone.

Appearing between the third and fourth series[28] the cast had expanded to a large ensemble of brilliant roles and everyone gets some great lines here from Forbes Collins' horrible King John to the wet Guy of Gisbourne (Ramsay Gilderdale) but it's the brilliantly naive guards Gary and Graeme (future best-selling crime author Mark Billingham and David Lloyd) who get the best gags (*"We can take out the whole of Worksop", "I wouldn't want to take out Gladys", "I wouldn't mind if she kept her teeth in..."*) as they train a new savage guard named Gavin who just so happens to be four years old. It's far from the series' high point but its placing as part of Christmas Eve's teatime schedule was high praise indeed proving its timeless, jubilant quality for all ages. That said, a line about "servicing muck spreaders" may have caused a few parents at home to choke on their mince pies…

---

[28] The 1992 copyright date would suggest it had been filmed the previous year. The fourth and final series would begin 5th January 1994.

Friday, 24th December, 1993

10pm: Camp Christmas (Channel 4)

"Welcome to Camp Christmas where all the guests are gay."

With a vibe of Val Doonican turned up to a thousand "Camp Christmas" is a quirky but celebratory hour of telly as pretty much every out star in 1993 appears in this new take on a very old style of special. The hosts are singers Vince Clarke from Erasure and Melissa Etheridge who give it their all starting with a bontempi-tastic[29] Christmas medley on a snowy set before heading inside a suitably old school log cabin complete with a Julian Clary-voiced reindeer head on the wall.

Inside the cabin is a mingling of faces including director Derek Jarman in his last television appearance, comic Simon Fanshawe (*"What's the worst present you can give a lesbian for Christmas? Martina's phone number with one digit wrong…"*), the late footballer Justin Fashanu in a Cosby-rific sweater, Australian entertainment sensation Bob Downe and Lea DeLaria - now best known as Big Boo in "Orange Is The New Black" - who does a routine about Italian Christmases. Lily Savage and Polly Perkins arrive later as caterers and there's a visit from a filthy Father Christmas who sounds a lot like Stephen Fry. There's even room for Col. Margarethe Cammermeyer who had recently been dismissed from the military for admitting to being gay during the shameful "don't ask, don't tell" period of US history and would soon be played by

---

[29] Vince Clarke was musical director accompanied by Heaven 17's Martyn Ware and the script was written by cabaret star Kit Hesketh-Harvey and Mark Trevorrow, Bob Downe himself.

Glenn Close in a 1995 movie "Serving in Silence". And can that really be Pam St Clement as a singing fairy on the Christmas tree?

It's a very international programme - Martina Navratilova calls in from Zurich, Amistead Maupin reads "A Christmas Carol" in San Francisco which leads us to Scrooge's Diner in New York being run by Quentin Crisp who talks of his childhood Christmases. You know you're watching something from a different era when the hosts have to explain Pride and the rainbow colours but, despite questions on the House of Commons about it around the time, it's a fairly tame broadcast to modern eyes and that's hopefully a positive thing. The idea that such a programme would be a controversial statement seems ridiculous now but as the producer Frances Dickenson said more recently: *"At that time the UK was a pretty unfriendly place for the LGBT community. Section 28 had become law, ignorance about HIV was rampant and homophobic attacks were common both on the streets and in the media. We decided we wanted to strike back with humour, snow and woolly jumpers."* I think they succeeded spectacularly.

Saturday, 25th December, 1993

7.00am: Chorlton in the Ice World (UK Gold)

Originally appearing on Boxing Day 1977 this was the sole special for the charming Cosgrove Hall animation "Chorlton and the Wheelies" about a cheerful dragon in a world of wheel-based inhabitants. Undoubtedly a smashing way to spend half an hour, it's the first of many archive Christmas programmes being shown by UK Gold throughout the day at a time where satellite TV rarely changed its line-up regardless of what the day was. Some lesser spotted stuff was chosen including a rare episode of children's comedy "Rentaghost", three 1970s editions of "Top Of The Pops" and sitcom antics in "Terry and June", "Rings on Their Fingers", "Are You Being Served?" and "No Place Like Home".

In contrast, Sky One's concession to the day was another showing of the miserable "Alf's Christmas Special" from seven years earlier while Sky Movies premiered "Star Trek VI: The Undiscovered Country". At least the newly launched Nickelodeon had a few tinsel-tinged programmes including the RL Stine penned puppet oddity "Christmas at Eureeka's Castle", a 1962 Mr Magoo one-off and whatever "Jason Donovan's Christmas Special" consisted of. They also had the adult political cartoon comedy "Capitol Critters" at 9am so swings and roundabouts I suppose?

Saturday, 25th December, 1993

11.45am: Inside the Wrong Trousers (BBC Two)

"Behind-the-scenes look at the work of animator Nick Park."

It's hard to imagine a time before the charming stop-motion double act of Wallace and Gromit were part of our lives. Despite only appearing in four shorts and a feature-length film[30], their adventures have been beloved by the world for as long as I care to remember…even if that memory only stretches back to Christmas

---

[30] Ok, so there was the "Cracking Contraptions" TV series. And the TellTale games. And about a thousand adverts but you know what I mean...

Eve 1990 when "A Grand Day Out" first appeared on Channel 4. Nick Park had begun the process of making it in 1982 but could only work on it part-time after being offered a job by Aardman Animations. Even Peter Sallis, who took just £50 for his time voicing Wallace, had forgotten recording his part when Park presented him with the finished product some seven years later.

By the time "The Wrong Trousers" was gearing up for its Boxing Day premiere on BBC2, "A Grand Day Out" had been nominated for Best Animated Short Film at the 1990 Academy Awards but it was tragically beaten by "Creature Comforts" made by...um, Nick Park. In this short warm-up film Park talks us through his sketch book and how an animation set is carefully lit and filmed. The intricate detail in these miniature rooms is breath-taking - something I can say from experience having seen the gorgeous museum set up close at the Media Museum in Bradford – and it's a captivating look at how animation works even if it's slow pace was most likely a big influence on that "Fast Show" sketch with the "Fancy a pint?" bloke.

From this Christmas onwards Wallace and Gromit have always felt part of the holiday season with follow-up "A Close Shave" appearing on Christmas Eve 1995 and the duo even appearing on the channel's '2' idents that year. The second time would be the charm for "The Wrong Trousers" at the Oscars and in 2000 the BFI placed it as the 18th best programme ever, nestled between "Absolutely Fabulous" and "The World at War". What would Gromit say about that?

Saturday, 25th December, 1993

3.00pm: The Alternative Queen's Message

"With Quentin Crisp at the Plaza"

The first of Channel 4's "alternative Christmas messages" featuring voices that had been relevant or had something to say about the year just passed. Appearing in his capacity as the "Englishman in New York", the 85 year old writer, performer and trail-blazing eccentric Crisp offered his opinions on his adopted country and the incumbent President Bill Clinton. Speaking in New York's famous Plaza Hotel he is damning about the idea of a welfare state (*"They watched many episodes of Sesame Street, and they wish for change. The trouble with this grand notion is that it will cost money. A lot of it!"*) but optimistic about New York (*"This city instantly embraced me, and I it."*) although his comments on the opposite sex (*"women have now decided to become people. This is a change for the worst. Women were nicer than people…"*) and the USA itself (*"America is not in a sufficiently secure position to bomb the world, so it has decided to save it, which may prove to be just as expensive, and will certainly take much longer"*) may

require a certain amount of tongue in cheek.

With Crisp filmed as part of Channel 4's "Christmas In New York" theme in 1993, the following year's "Black Christmas" theme sought the opinion of the Reverend Jesse Jackson. Jackson, who had made international news when he stood as a Presidential candidate for the Democrats in 1984 and 1988, spoke about moving politics and race relations forward. A message that never stops being relevant. This was followed in 1995 by former actress and model Brigitte Bardot in her role as an animal rights activist for "Beastly Christmas" week. 1996 proved how big a difference a year would make as Rory Bremner spoofed Diana, Princess of Wales' post-marriage independence (*"I'm still big, it's the monarchy that has got small."*) with a comic chat show called "The Time, The Palace". With her now 'The People's Princess' by 1997, a Shankhill teenager called Margaret Gibney spoke about peace in Northern Ireland which was still several months away from the Good Friday Agreement being agreed upon. Having already met with Tony Blair and Hillary Clinton that year, the 13-year old Belfast girl had made a name by writing to over 150 world leaders calling for an end to all wars.

Doreen and Neville Lawrence, the parents of murdered teenager Stephen Lawrence, spoke in 1998 about the need for governments to honour their son's name with stronger laws against racist and hate crimes, a message that remains eternal and necessary 22 years on. After that, it perhaps seems a strange choice to give the speech to Sacha Baron Cohen as "The 11'O Clock Show" character Ali G who had broken through that year despite being from one of the most hateful programmes ever broadcast.

The slot would continue until the present day with names from the world of entertainment (Sharon Osbourne, Adam Hills, a couple from TV's "Wife Swap") with those who had been through era-defining moments including a 9/11 survivor named Genelle Guzman, the former President of Iran Mahmoud Ahmadinejad, government whistle-blower Edward Snowden, survivors of the Grenfell Tower fire and Brendan Cox whose wife MP Jo Cox had been senselessly murdered in 2016. Sadly, perhaps due to channel choice or Channel 4's move into less controversial or ground-breaking television, these rarely have the impact many of them clearly deserve. The biggest reaction in years actually came in 2020 with The Queen herself deep faked with sophisticated technology and impressionist Debra Stephenson.

Sunday, 26th December, 1993

4.25pm: Peter and the Wolf - a Prokofiev Fantasy (BBC Two)

"Conductor Claudio Abbado conducts…"

Whereas it might be said that I know more about Terrorvision than Toscanini, I've always enjoyed the wealth of classical music that Christmas invariably brought to the small screen, especially when they tried something new or quirky with the staging. Here the "symphonic fairy tale for children" gets the rubber-faced treatment as "Spitting Image" co-creator Roger Law directs - in conjunction with Christopher Swann and Steve Bendelack - a range of humans, puppets and weird hybrids of both. Narrating the tale is Mr Sting in puppet form[31] alongside the late Roy Hudd who puts in a career highlight dual role as both Prokofiev and 'Roy Hudd' preparing for the role in a word-free world of puppets, including a disconcerting one of himself.

A number of recognisable puppets from the ITV satire series can be seen throughout including the Royals up in the box but mostly this is an all new cast of animals and oddballs for Peter, played by 11 year old newcomer Henry Feagins, to interact with. Of note are

---

[31] Sting had been a previous collaborator with "Spitting Image" in 1984 lending his voice to a powerful reworking of "Every Breath You Take".

enormously frightening full body versions of The Three Stooges which must have been lost on most kids who weren't already hidden behind the sofa. Sharp-eyed viewers might be able to spot a 27-year old Toby Jones in the human side of the acting troupe as part of the Théâtre de Complicité before he went on to be the best one in everything ever made.

For years "Peter and the Wolf", with each animal in the tale is represented by a specific instrument, has been one of those "no you like classical music really!" shows that has always been used to try get kids into something a bit more substantial than their Bros tapes. Directed with a good sense of pace and urgency, the Sunday afternoon slot possibly didn't help focus its younger viewers - especially if they'd already had lunch or had noticed "Superman III" was on the other side. But for those who don't nod off, it's a beautiful, eerie and interesting take on an oft-produced story. It's easy to see why the "Spitting Image" producers were looking to expand outside the initial series which by now was long past its best, having long lost the shock or impact it once had.

Tuesday 28th December 1993

10.45pm: The Comedians Christmas Cracker (ITV)

"A special party of non-stop laughter to celebrate 21 years."

Every time there's a documentary about British television comedy made, the chances are a clip from 70s stand-up vehicle "The Comedians" will appear to show the lows of how TV in that decade could be. A huge prime-time hit for ITV between 1971 and 1974, the incredibly cheap talent showcase could be quite tame but equally could also be frequently sexist, homophobic, racist and pretty much anything else you could imagine. These were acts straight from the working men's clubs and it made instant celebrities out of comics like Stan Boardman, Jim Bowen, Frank Carson, Ken Goodwin, Charlie Williams, Bernard Manning and Mick Miller. Despite the rise of alternative comedy, the old-style stand up never went away even if the TV bookings stopped and the early 90s boom in 'blue' live sets recorded for home video meant comics no longer had to temper their acts for television leading to acts like Manning, "Chubby" Brown and Jethro selling in huge amounts. Which perversely then made telly want a cut of it leading to a five-episode "The Comedians" revival in 1992. That time it was not a hit and so this post-watershed "tribute" to 21 years since the original series[32] would therefore be its last hoorah on terrestrial telly. Unlike the original series that cut quickly between stand-ups with no audience shots, this is a live stage show with all the comics in the audience like a roast of…well, less a person and more the notions of common sense and decency. Throughout the set clips of the original series are shown, including an 18-year-old Les Dennis who regrettably returns in 1993 to do a knees-up singsong to the "Bonanza" theme. No really.

It's fairly domesticated considering what was now appearing on video but there's a strange, depressing energy to the affair as if being transmitted from a club trapped in amber for two decades with the same old gags and routines. Mick Miller at least attempts to mention something beyond the Heath administration with a

---

[32] There'd be no series of "The Comedians" in 1975-1978, 1981-1983, 1986-1991 or any official shows after this. A 40th anniversary show was recorded in Blackpool in 2011 for DVD.

silly piece about recent film westerns before the only black comedian of the original run Charlie Williams takes the stage to talk about being mistaken for Nelson Mandela. Ken Goodwin is happily much dafter than his contemporaries (*"My pal bought a box of After Eights and he died at seven thirty..."*) but the real surprise for me was Colin Crompton who was more cerebral (*"Morecambe... it's a sort of cemetery with lights"*) than the thundering chairman character I'd seen on similar 1970s variety showcase "The Wheeltappers and Shunters Social Club". Thankfully he wasn't here to ruin that image as he'd done the decent thing and died in 1985.

Thursday, 30th December, 1993

10.10pm: An Evening with Lee Evans (Channel 4)

"Lee Evans won this year's Perrier Award and, at 28, is widely regarded as British comedy's Next Big Thing."

More stand-up of a very different kind here as television began its ceaseless attempts at working out what to do with Lee Evans on television. A breathless, manic and inventive act who'd become a hit with comedy fans but not yet broken through to the national attention he soon would get. This is a fairly straightforward best of from his 1993 Edinburgh show although an opening sequence does feature impressive cameos from an uncredited Jack Dee and Bruce Forysth plus a short but very funny silent sketch fighting with the conductor (Boothby Graffoe) of a small constantly-playing orchestra. Telly audiences also got one of the first chances to see his literal mime rendition of Queen's "Bohemian Rhapsody" which has since become a genuine bona fide classic.

Friday, 31st December, 1993

6.30pm: Lulu's Big Show (BBC Two)

"Singing some of her favourite songs and joined by surprise guests"

7.05pm: Opening Shot: Suede (Channel 4)

"This follows the band and their fans, particularly the Suede Family, a group of eccentrics who hang out with their heroes."

Two fairly different slices of breakthrough pop from 1993. For Lulu it had been another bite of the cherry after her first hit single in seven years ("Independence") before cannily being asked by Take That to sing on their cover of "Relight My Fire". Still only 45 at this point it's a solid reminder of how long and enduring much of Lulu's career had been, even if she didn't do any of her "Secret Diary of Adrian Mole" (series two ONLY) lines now I think of it.

Suede, however, are new. Shining, hip shaking, lank-haired newness and this short documentary follows them on tour whilst shadowed by their devoted teenage fans for whom the poppy yet idiosyncratic Suede were clearly made. The perfect crossover band with the tight trousers and big choruses of pop but the mystique and danger of indie which was at a really curious junction where the fanzines, Beechwood Music compilations and charity shop chic had not yet given way to Britpop and bulging big label wallets. It's also an noteworthy place to check in with Suede who don't yet seem jaded with fame and lead singer Brett Anderson chatting openly about being a teenage Crass fan. With the guitarist acrimoniously leaving in 1994 its intriguing to note one moment where several fans blank Bernard Butler as they swarm around Anderson stood next to him.

There's pretention in spades of course as there seems to be with any young indie band in their early years but the music still sounds bloody brilliant with an early unfinished version of "Stay Together" excerpted towards the end. Everett True from "Melody Maker" appears to say the press loved Suede because they were a throwback to the glam of 1973 which the fans vehemently disagree with "because they didn't even live through the 70s". It's hard not to smile at the young fans though when they talk about singing "The Next Life" in RE class as the band look on delighted.

Saturday, 1st January, 1994

5.40pm: Stars in Their Eyes Special (ITV)

"The show that gives its guests a chance at singing stardom."

A show full of Christmas songs performed just after Christmas by former "Stars In Their Eyes" winners doing songs not even by the artist they're best at pretending to do. Confused? You should be.

The tone is set with host Matthew Kelly playing the "Coronation Street" theme on his digital watch before our first returning singer and tonight Matthew he's going to be...sigh, Gary Glitter. It's hard to say if the silver-clad hunks popping out of present boxes throughout helped or hindered "Another Rock N Roll Christmas" which was preceded by an anecdote about featuring the unfortunate line *"The police came and I had to explain why I was dressed as Gary Glitter"* to which Kelly replies *"I'd have locked you up!"*

Next up is a Dodgy David Essex up with some laugh-free anecdotes about owning ferrets before "A Winter's Tale" sets the nation's grandmas a-fluttering. But it's what happens next which set my jaw to drop as the producers have clearly run out of winners who perform singers with Christmas songs in their back catalogue and so three female finalists come on as a Charlatan Cilla Black, Make-Believe Madonna and Counterfeit Cyndi Lauper to sing "Santa Baby" which is a song that sadly suits none of their voices. It gets worse as A Sham Sinatra, A Knock-Off Nat King Cole and A um... Mountebank Marc Almond duet similarly on "Zat You Santa Claus?"

The pearl in the pop shell comes later with an up-tempo rocking medley as Mock Meatloaf gives his all to "Rudolf the Red Nosed Reindeer" before a Bogus Billy Idol massacres "All I Want For Christmas Is My Two Front Teeth" and Ersatz Elton joins them for "Run Rudolph Run" managing to sound more like Gilbert Gottfried on Mogadon than the Rocket Man himself. My favourite however is surely the Affected Axl Rose who squawks his best through "Santa Claus Is Coming To Town" whilst clearly dying a little inside. Then the whole thing ends with that classic Christmas double-act Bing and erm...Elvis.

Its cringe-worthy, it's ridiculous and it made me near choke with laughter but I can't deny I had a lot of fun watching it and unlike later editions they didn't spend twenty minutes finding out the life stories of each contestant. And compared to the bloated TV singing contests in the last fifteen years, it's like the Last Night of The Proms.

Saturday, 1st January, 1994

9.00pm: The Paul Calf Video Diary (BBC Two)

…"I'm not wearing dead man's pants", "Is it luminous?", "If she's not careful, she's going to break that coffee table", "My God they're big", "I'm going as The Incredible Hulk", "It's an erection", "Nicholas Witchell...Nicholas Witchell...Nicholas Witchell...", "In the toilet?", "You've got shit shoes on, you shitty shoe bastard", "mam, she called me a bastard", "Schopenhauer, where are you now?", "Who's Kafka kicking?", "It was a paradox, y'daft cow!", "I'd rather see Dave Lee Travis play Macbeth", "PENIS!", "Have yer got any Suede?", "fat blobby bastard Bob", "Bag of shite"…..

1994

Highest Rated Programme: The strongest battle in some time saw BBC One's "One Foot in the Grave" go head to head with ITV's "Heartbeat" in the 9pm slot with the victor being….well, Victor again with 15.14 million punters to 13.79m for Nick Berry's 60s copperin'. The third channel get in the top ten twice more with "Blind Date" (11.96m) and "Coronation Street" (12.38m) but the combined might of "EastEnders" (14.23m), "Keeping Up Appearances" (13.69m) and Victoria Wood: Live In Your Own Home (13.39m) was too powerful for the plucky programmer.

Big Films on the BBC: Your mileage may vary on "Robin Hood: Prince Of Thieves" which takes up a large chunk of Christmas night, not to mention 14 million viewers. "The Addams Family" and a pre-watershed showing of the 15-certificate "Kindergarten Cop" take us through Boxing Day and "Dick Tracy" pops up on the 27th. Sadly not timed to follow on after that for a saucy Madge double bill is "In Bed With Madonna" on the 29th December over on Two. There's also "Thelma and Louise", Demi Moore in "The Butcher's Wife" and an entire evening is given over to the biggest acquisition - Oliver Stone's "JFK".

Big Films on ITV: It's a fairly bare cupboard at ITV Towers with 1986 Goldie Hawn comedy "Wildcats" slung out in prime-time on Christmas Eve but a Disney double-bill of "Mary Poppins" and a debuting "Sleeping Beauty" on the big day itself is more welcome… unless you're in one the regions that decided to swap Mary for "The Empire Strikes Back" instead. "Honey I Shrunk The Kids" is on Boxing Day though its 10:15pm end time seems not quite in the spirit of the audience it was intended for.

Big Films on Channel 4: Terry Gilliam's incorrectly battered "The Adventures of Baron Munchausen" is one of Four's few new showings as is a re-mastered version of Orson Welles' 1951 "Othello" which probably wouldn't fly too well in the current age. Danny Kaye gets his own mini season of films during the daytime and there's some "Chinese Ghost Stories" which eagle eyed viewers will spot is almost identical to the season Channel 4 ran four years earlier. Spooky!

Oh That Queen's Speech: More lovely war dead remembrances as the D-Day landings were commemorated. She'd also been over to Russia for a bit of a potter round some shops and the odd yard of Old Ivanovich's 100 Proof Eyebrow Melter.

For The Kids: A poor show from BBC One on the run up to Christmas with programmes like "Playdays" and "Thunderbirds" hoyed over to BBC Two. Later "Why Don't You…?" makes its final appearance in a Christmas line-up which feels like the sad but inevitable end of an era. ITV have got…yes, more "He-Man" plus the 1991 animation "James Bond Jr." about 007's tedious nephew and the freaky Australian pre-school "Bananas in Pyjamas".

The Pops: Who's on hosting duties this year? Why, it's only Flippin' Take That! With the world now aware they had actual personalities, it was a solid choice even when their closest rivals East 17 are 1994's Christmas No.1, something they'd been denied by a multi-coloured Noel Edmonds folly the previous year. Mostly videos and repeat performances here but making the effort were new pop favourites Eternal, the inevitable Whigfield, Let Loose with the mighty "Crazy For You", the appallingly named All-4-One. D: bloody Ream, Mariah Carey and a down-tempo slow dance from Stiltskin. But don't worry, Wet Wet Wet are back with…oh you know. The That are also in concert on Channel 4 before – ick – "The Frank Sinatra of the 90s" Harry Connick Jr. in the evening. The artist formerly known as The Pop Singer Prince rolls in later at 12:55am with "The Beautiful Experience" described as "explosive new music, provocative dancing…rock at the cutting edge". So probably no jug band bogling then.

Radio Times Cover: Barry Norman picks his favourites from another 700 movie options as an ugly family sit staring into different corners of the room. The particular old timey nature of this one is due to it being an update by Bob Venables of a 1924 cover but with "Jaws Special Edition" style updates to the clothing and cigarettes carefully removed whereas the gramophone is replaced by a good old fashioned massive barcode. Still £1.30 to you pal.

TV Times Cover: Santa's back, now waving from his sleigh. Probably thinking about how the TV Times with its 20 page film pull-out is still five pence cheaper than the Radio Times.
New Year's Daze: Clive James puts in a final New Year's appearance for BBC One before he heads back off to ITV but the following "Hogmanay Live" invites you to stick around for Paul Coia, Runrig and "members of the Strathclyde Police Pipe Band". Two bursts of footage from an ill-advised "Woodstock '94" sandwich the second Hootenanny with guests Steve Winwood and

Blur. Over on Channel 4 was "When Johnny Cash Went To Glastonbury". Hope he played some music when he was there. Seems a waste otherwise.

Theme Nights: BBC Two leant into its popular new import "The X Files" with "Weird Night" running from 8.35pm to 7:30am and featuring "The Fortean Review of the Year", a documentary about the traditional American carnival freak shows, George A Romero's take on the vampire genre "Martin" and a 1970 short film by David Lynch. Channel 4's next theme week was "Black Christmas" with everything from documentaries on jungle music to the last episode of much-loved sitcom "Desmond's".

Wouldn't Happen Now: There's a maudlin Christmas Day double-bill of "Noel's Christmas Presents" and "Animal Hospital Christmas" on BBC One right after the Queen that presumably contributed to a rise in seasonal razor blade sales.

New For '95: The correct answer is of course "The Glam Metal Detectives" of course but ITV had the twin barrel assault of "Kavanagh QC" and Shane Richie's "Lucky Numbers" in its first week of 1995. But for many the true voice of 1995 was the host of new BBC One quiz show "Timekeepers" Bill Dod with his eternally beloved catchphrase "you are right".

Is The Sound Of Music On? No, the BBC had already blown it at Easter, the mad fools!

Friday, 23rd December, 1994

12.35am: Beavis and Butt-Head (Channel 4)

"The animated heavy metal anti-heroes offer their unique opinions..."

It shouldn't be funny to watch two idiots trying to make "wood" jokes as they watch a video of a roaring fire, especially when one misunderstands and says "penis" to "join in the conversation" but I laughed as much re-watching "A Very Special Christmas With Beavis and Butt-Head" as I did the first time I saw it a quarter of a decade ago.

The boys love Christmas because *"you get to sit around and watch TV"* and unlike their usual stories where they occasionally leave the house watching TV is all they do here with a whole half hour devoted to them commenting over Yule-themed music videos and the odd fireplace tableau. Their comments range from the joyfully dumb (Frosty the Snowman becomes "Testes The Snowman") to the surprisingly savvy (*"I know what this is*", says Butt-Head of the original "Do They Know It's Christmas?", *"...this is when a bunch of rich people get together and ask for money..."*) with an internal logic of the sort you get in the middle of the night (*"If you eat your own boogers, does that make you, like, one of those cannabists?"*) Musically, David Bowie and Bing Crosby are met by horror while The California Raisins pass muster because *"they look like turds"* and the "Dance of the Sugarplum Fairies" is cool because it *"sounds like Ozzy"*. "Cashing in on Christmas" by Bad News also initially goes down well due to a scene where Den Dennis (Nigel Planer) sings on the toilet. A phenomenon from the first crudely-animated, ultra-violent episode "Beavis and Butt-Head" were the big shocking thing for 1993 just as "The Simpsons" had been in 1989 and "South Park" would be later. Unlike most of those shows, it's kept a lot of his bite due to smart writing, not hanging round long enough to get boring and a naive joy the characters take in everything - positivity we could all do with right now.

Saturday, 24th December, 1994

9.00pm: Don't Forget Your Toothbrush (Channel 4)

"Chris Evans offers the chance of a holiday trip for two of the studio audience in another edition of the live entertainment show."

One of the shortest lived shows (26 episodes in just over a year) with the biggest impacts, "Don't Forget Your Toothbrush" managed to get the attention, press and admiration a channel would sell their souls for in the modern age. Then again, so much of the soul and presentation of this fast-paced mix of game show, music show and comedy show can be found in the roots of pretty much every light entertainment show of the past 25 years from "The National Lottery Live" to "Ant and Dec's Saturday Night Takeaway".

With the memories fading and Chris Evans forever vacillating between 'good presenter' and 'irritating git', I felt apprehensive about returning to this show I'd loved as a teenager. It was as much a part of my Saturday night as "The New Adventures of Superman", "Gladiators" and them late films on the German channel that I probably shouldn't talk about. No time to think here through as we whip through a raucous audience wrapping presents, stuffing turkeys and judging presents before a Jools

Holland-led boogie woogie rockin' "Silent Night" sets the tempo for the next hour. It's hard to blame the crowd for getting too restless when any of them could win a dream holiday or even a random surprise at the drop of a hat[33]. But before all that the ideas fly by as a remote control turkey randomly appears, someone guesses drinks being fired from a hose (she's clueless to all of them), Evans prank calls a hotel in Jerusalem asking for a room for Joseph and Mary (they don't get it), there's a sprout tombola ("Rustle my Brussels!") and a Somerset household gets tons of snow dumped on their lawn as a treat. The special guest is Roy Wood looking like Professor Denzil Dexter from "The Fast Show" aged anywhere from 30 to 75 and you'll never guess what he's singing! That's right - "Angel Fingers"....wait no, it's the Christmas one! The all-female brass section sounds particularly fine, shame the rest of the musicians from Jools' band aren't quite as on it. After that, Roy's dragged into a 'Superfan' quiz answering questions about his own career. The episode concludes with the big "Light Your Lemon" game where a couple can win an immediate trip to either St Lucia or St Ives. And because it's Christmas, of course they get the good one.

After that we all have a sing song to "Merry Xmas (War Is Over)" and then it's over leaving you sat breathless, slightly dizzy and unsure what you've just seen. Not that it mattered to Evans who had just two more months of "Toothbrush" to complete before taking a small islands-worth of cash to host the Radio 1 Breakfast show and invent yet more head-spinning TV for Channel Four.

---

33 In this episode everyone received a frozen turkey and a bottle of vodka, although I do wonder how many turkeys were left on the night bus home…

Sunday, 25th December, 1994

5.30pm: Zig & Zag's Christmas Special (Channel 4)

"The playful puppets Zig and Zag cause mayhem as self-styled comedy police, ready to book anyone who isn't funny."

And here are Chris' old mates off "The Big Breakfast" who had almost become as famous as him despite being ratty puppets supposedly from the Planet Zog. This half hour pilot sees Zig and Zag in their non-TV job as "Entertainment Cops" bringing to justice the worst of light entertainment scum. The 90s seemed obsessed with making parodies of 70s cop shows and this was another complete with pastiche titles, daft posing and humming of "The Sweeney" theme. The brothers are sent by their boss (Richard Wilson) to stop Eamonn Holmes producing "criminal entertainment" in the form of his "Country Christmas Spectacular". The best bits of their breakfast interviews were always the interactions with celebrities who hadn't a clue what they'd let themselves in for and here Jean-Claude Van Damme is perhaps the least likely cameo, although an in character Helen Mirren as Jane Tennison comes close. Less surprising are Tom O Connor, Eric Bristow, Frank Bruno, Dale Winton, Kenneth "the landlord from Only Fools and Horses" MacDonald, Christopher Biggins and Chas 'n' Dave.

Joined by oddly forgotten teen celebrity Alex Langdon, there's lots of running about and daft jokes before a conclusion on HMS Belfast with the puppet brothers dressed for some reason as Brucie and Rosemarie Ford. The day is saved and the duo use the opportunity to put on their own Christmas show featuring a ragga country song named "Turn Your Landing Light which punters could helpfully find on the B-side of Zig and Zag's real life single "Dem Girls, Dem Girls" which was presently nestled at No. 8 in the Christmas chart.

A similar series "Zig and Zag's Dirty Deeds" would turn up in 1996 but it was a little too late to catch the peak of the Zogly brothers' fame[34]. Always better live and unleashed, they've never really gone away, missus.

Sunday, 25th December, 1994

10.00pm: Robin Williams in the Wild with Dolphins (ITV)

"Comic actor Robin Williams embarks on a fascinating tropical quest to learn more about the legendary intelligence of dolphins."

A novel way to give up on your Christmas Day schedule, ITV. This imported documentary from America's PBS is a pleasant enough hour with Williams surrounded by gorgeous photography of dolphins and the Bahamas but it feels more a Boxing Day teatime kind of pick rather than 10pm on the big night itself. Especially with a new Victoria Wood special on the other side! Once he gets all the impressions out of his system Robin is a decent front-person for a series like this and quickly allows himself to be won over by the breadbins of the sea. After appearing in

---

[34] Much more worth discovering from around the same time is the short lived "Zig and Zag's Zogazine" an anarchic Fleetway comic which parodied everything from Bowie to film noir, horror, fairy tales and comics themselves.

some of the biggest films of the 90s, Williams had experienced a quiet 1994 with only one big film in cinemas - the Bill Forsyth ("Gregory's Girl", "Local Hero" etc.) written and directed "Being Human" which flopped in part due to studio meddling.

"In The Wild" was an irregular series where celebrities would get to front their own show with different wildlife and included such combinations as "Wolves with Timothy Dalton", "Tigers with Bob Hoskins", "The Elephants of India with Goldie Hawn", "The Galapagos Islands with Richard Dreyfuss", "Pandas with Debra Winger" and "Mongolian Horsemen with Julia Roberts".

Monday, 26th December, 1994

10.30am: Saved by the Bell Hawaiian Style (Channel 4)

"A feature-length episode of the teen comedy."

The 90s was a particularly good time to be a teenager. From "Beverly Hills 90210" to "Dawson's Creek" it felt like the decade that wanted to reach teen audiences and listen to what they had to say. I mean, what they had to say was effectively bollocks - I speak very much from experience... but the likes of "Byker Grove", "Pugwall", "My So Called Life", "Teenage Health Freak," youth rights series "Wise Up", some new soap called "Hollyoaks" and the majority of BBC Two's "DEF II" strand felt - ahem - for young adults by young adults.

So out of all these worthy, ground-breaking and interesting series why is it that "Saved By The Bell" - an incredibly light high school comedy from America with life lessons forever being learned in the most clunking obvious way - remains a beloved part of so many people's memories including, if I'm honest, my own.

We were quite a way behind the American broadcasts with this TV movie romp about the Bayside High teens pulling together to save a hotel from a greedy real-estate developer originally airing in the November of 1992 on NBC. This would be a precursor to a brand-new evening spin-off series "Saved by the Bell: the College Years" which would begin the week after on Channel 4 despite already being cancelled in the US and wrapped up with a second telemovie "Wedding In Las Vegas".

Despite its Day-Glo colours and early nineties obsessions "Saved By The Bell" would go into a similar repeat cycle as "The Fresh Prince of Bel Air" joined by the totally unmemorable "Saved By The Bell: The New Class" which actually lasted three years longer than its predecessor and then a parade of identikit re-workings of the same premise from the same producer such as "California Dreams" ("Saved By The Bell" but it's a band), "Hang Time" ("Saved By The Bell" but its basketball), "USA High" ("Saved By The Bell" but it's a boarding school), "City Guys" ("Saved By The Bell" but they're different colours), "All About Us" ("Saved By The Bell" but it's just female characters) and "Malibu, CA" ("Saved By The Bell" but it's...um, in Malibu.)

You can't keep a good preppie down and with the current nostalgia clock being stuck around 1992 its little surprise that a revival of "Saved By The Bell" began at the end of 2020 with several of the original series main characters' children starting at their old alma mater. Luckily it is both bodacious and genuinely excellent.

Tuesday, 27th December, 1994

8.00pm: The Bible (Sky One)

"The Old Testament story of Abraham and the trials he endures"

Yes, the Bible! Look busy! This was the first of a promised full run of the Bible's best from Abraham's search for the promised land of Canaan here to ol' "Doubting" Thomas in 2001. Seventeen volumes would be produced ultimately for billionaire Ted Turner's TNT network with 27 parts in total. With Richard Harris as Abram/Abraham and Barbara Hershey as his wife-slash-half-sister Sarah, these were not cheaply knocked out affairs but fans of lovely Jesus would have to wait until 1999 for his own film where he would be played by Jeremy Sisto off of "Six Feet Under".

Wednesday, 28th December, 1994

9.15pm: The Lenny Henry Christmas Show (BBC One)

"More fun with the larger-than-life Lenny Henry."

Despite most people mentioning Morecambe and Wise, Mike Yarwood or The Two Ronnies as constants on British TV at Christmas, Lenny Henry rarely gets a mention. 1994 brought a different kind of show for Lenny, a post-watershed special shot 'as live' in front of an audience with more of a hip nightclub feel and a less family-targeted vibe. Much as he had reinvented himself from naive "New Faces" winner to kids favourite on "TISWAS" and again for "Three of a Kind" then his own series, here was yet another shift to keep people on their toes. It was a bold move not least because Henry had dropped all of this popular characters for a new bunch of more topical ones including corrupt and rich African ruler King Ade, hopeless Welsh rappers TWA - Taffies with Attitude and the RuPaul-esque Amazon model Deeva who teases the stunned audience. The only sketch not performed on stage is a spot on Blaxploitation spoof with a guest appearance by 'Jason King' himself, Peter Wyngarde.

Always a voice for pushing black culture to the forefront, Len uses his new line-up to show a more relevant take on the modern world that was unashamedly proud of its heritage. With music from Salt 'N' Pepa and Dina Carroll this was an intriguing if American-influenced new look from a face we'd known for nearly two decades. A series using this same style would launch on Saturday nights the following April but struggled to make the impact of his early work. Not that it seemed to bother Henry who continues being interesting and offending the right people to this day.

Thursday, 29th December, 1994

7.20pm: The Marriage of Figaro (BBC Two)

"The story of a sex-mad Eurocrat who's trying to sleep with his servant, his frustrated aristocratic wife and her toyboy..."

Another intriguing attempt to make an established opera relevant to modern audiences. No rubber puppets this time but a new translation of Lorenzo da Ponte's libretto that would play up the farcical elements of Mozart's already naughty comic opera. The perpetually randy Count Almaviva of the original is now Sir Cecil, a sleazy Tory bureaucrat who has his sights set on bedding the maid Susanna before her marriage to Cecil's valet Figaro. With the plot sounding like something from "EastEnders" the producer and director Geoff Posner, best known for his comedy work on everything from "Not The Nine O'Clock News" to "Little Britain", plays up to this with a stark sitcom style set with characters bounding and out of the scenes singing the new English lines which had been translated by Tony Britten and Nicholas Broadhurst. Even Nigel Planer turns up as Antonio, the gardener described in the book as "a smelly and cantankerous old git".

It's a brilliantly funny and fast-paced production that takes the four acts of the original opera and fits them into three nightly programmes. With the reworked Count character now a subtle pastiche of MP Alan Clark whose first volume of sensational diaries had been released in 1993, it's a topical reworking with a great cast clearly having the time of their lives that kept me watching. And with Tory sleaze scandals never too far away, it looks certainly to retain a lot of that relevancy for years to come.

Friday, 30th December, 1994

9.30pm: French and Saunders Christmas Special (BBC One)

10.10pm: A B'Stard Exposed (BBC One)

Two channel-hopping specials for the price of one! Originating on BBC Two and ITV respectively, "French and Saunders" and "The New Statesman" had both arrived in 1987 as starring vehicles for former members of the Comic Strip comedy club. The man behind the outrageously appalling Alan Beresford B'Stard MP, Rik

Mayall, had been a star since breaking through as the naive West Midlands investigative reporter Kevin Turvey on BBC2 comedy revue "A Kick Up The Eighties". Dawn French and Jennifer Saunders had taken slightly longer to become household names despite guest spots on "The Young Ones", "Saturday Live" and their own ITV sitcom "Girls on Top". Considered cuddly beloved figureheads now, French and Saunders were able to shock just as any of their male contemporaries in what was becoming known as alternative comedy with their first TV half hour (as part of Channel 4's new talent showcase "The Entertainers") being moved from its usual 8:30pm spot to after 11 due to the sexual nature of their act and in particular the use of the word "clitoris".

"The New Statesman" was coming to a close after four series which had seen the openly atrocious Alan attempt everything from arming the police to becoming Lord Protector of the entire United Kingdom. Indeed, the character was so rotten that he could only be played by someone as charming as Rik. Mayall would remain a beloved figure until his insanely early death in 2014 aged just 56, but this was end of the adventures for B'stard until a canny stage revival in the 00s. French and Saunders however were home and would become a huge part of Christmas on BBC One over the next two decades with the wonderful "Celebrity Christmas Puddings" in 2002 and 2017's semi-retrospective "300 Years of French and Saunders" appearing on the 25th.

All have since had National Treasure statuses bestowed upon them now beside names like Alexei Sayle, Adrian Edmondson, Robbie Coltrane and Sandi Toksvig but it's always good to remember how they were once total outsiders putting on their own show but, more importantly, bloody funny each of them are.

1995

Highest Rated Programme: Things were back on a more even keel this year with ITV just sneaking in one programme to the Christmas Day top ten and it'll be no surprise to learn its "Coronation Street" with 11.8 million. Soap viewers were 'treated' to not one but two episodes of "EastEnders" averaging about 16m but once again "One Foot In The Grave" was the winner for over 17 million households.

Big Films on the BBC: I mean how do you argue with a BBC One season that contains the first TV broadcasts of "Problem Child 2", "Beethoven" AND "Carry On Columbus"?!? Easily but still… Christmas Day featured the disappointing "Hook" and the probably not at all suitable for the time "Indecent Proposal" sharing space. BBC Two's first big film of the season is Antonio Banderas' English language debut "The Mambo Kings" followed by grim British thriller "The Hawk", epic retelling of Chinese history "Farewell My Concubine", Jan Švankmajer's eerie puppet retelling of the "Fault" legend and Robert Altman's satire of the movie industry "The Player".

Big Films on ITV: Some truly terrible festive flops during the day such as miserable Fred Savage TV movie "Christmas on Division Street", the self-explanatory "A Mom For Christmas" and the fantastically named "Mrs 'Arris Goes To Paris" with Angela Lansbury from 1992. "Sister Act" is the big Christmas film while Lenny Henry's Hollywood turn "True Identity" is…not.

Big Films on Channel 4: The classic "Charlotte Rampling takes a chimp as a lover" tropes appear in 1986's "Max Mon Amour" and the animal fun continues in Channel 4's "Beastly Christmas" season with "Leon The Pig Farmer", the Pinter-scripted comedy "Turtle Diary", misery classic "Kes", "Tarzan, The Ape Man", the always welcome post-apocalyptic comedy "A Boy and His Dog".

Oh That Queen's Speech: 1995 was the official year of some fine remembering of VE Day. The Queen also told us about a very special nun named Sister Ethel helping children in South Africa and ended with Christ's quote "Blessed be the peacemakers" as if she'd never even see "Life of Brian" or owt.

For The Kids: A bit of stuff on every terrestrial channel at one time or another with ITV's "Batman The Animated Series", BBC One cracking open the "Charlie Brown and Snoopy Show" and strange detective comedy "Jim Henson's Dog City" the pick of the pack. And yes, the now five years old "The New Adventures of He-Man" is still there at 9:25am.

The Pops: 1995 had been a successful year for unusual TOTP hosts – even Lee and Herring had popped up in May – and they didn't come more peculiar a pairing than Jack Dee and Bjork here. Despite being thought of now as the year of Britpop, the show represented what it was actually like with N-Trance, Boyzone, The Outhere Brothers and Simply Red on hand to do a turn alongside Blur, Pulp and Oasis - the latter a repeat of their cheeky "Roll With It" performance where Noel and Liam swapped places in order to try distract the audience from how terrible the single was. Blur also show up on Channel 4 as their 1994 "Showtime" concert pepped up many a late present unwrapping session. On ITV, Take That at Earls Court becomes their first "Pops" spoiler in years which may explain why TOTP was stepped back to 12:55pm.

Radio Times Cover: Back to 'Santa face' as an incredibly ruddy St. Nick holds a clapperboard to promote the EIGHT 'UNDRED FILLUMS on television that tinselled two weeks! Up to £1.50.

TV Times Cover: Old grinning zany Santa looks gormlessly into the readers' homes. Waiting. Just waiting. It's now twenty pence cheaper than its old rival but can still only offer thirteen cars to be won - twelve less than 1992. BOO!

New Year's Daze: Angus Deayton takes over from Clive James to provide much the same service in "The End of the Year Show" on BBC One before "Hogmanay Live" with the power duo of Gordon Kennedy and Lorraine Kelly introducing Edwyn Collins, Big Country, Eddi Reader and Gary Glitt…you know what never mind. On Two, the third Hootenanny is preceded by a TOTP2 special "Britpop: Then and Now" which celebrates a year of some indie getting in the chart as Menswear, Cast and Supergrass rub shoulders with The Hollies, The Kinks and Them There Beatles. Channel 4 weren't letting Jools claim all the New Year boogies as the Mark Radcliffe and Jo Whiley hosted "The White Room" saw viewers into 1996 with top tier line-up including Oasis, David Bowie, P M Dawn, Lou Reed and Pulp. Shame it'd be cancelled before the next New Year.

Theme Nights: No big spectaculars this year but Channel 4 have an animal themed week with "Beastly Christmas" while BBC Two continue their "BBC 100" season of the greatest films of all time.

Wouldn't Happen Now: I mean, I'm not putting my money entirely against it but I'm fairly sure that "Songs of Praise on Ice" from the Ice Arena at Blackpool Pleasure Beach on the 31st December was a definite novelty when it comes to the faith based telly staple. The musical special "Dannii on Safari" featuring a 'resting between hits' younger Minogue in Tanzania was equally a blessed one-off.

New For '96: "Our Friends in the North" on BBC Two is the biggest January newcomer even if "The Demon Headmaster" and "Hetty Wainthropp" might take umbrage with that with both beginning on January 3rd. BBC One are also gearing up to pinch "The X Files" from their sister channel and ITV launched totally forgotten Air Ambulance drama "Call Red" on January 8th.

Is The Sound Of Music On? Yes! BBC Two showed it on the 29th December at 5.15pm. Hitler is defeated once more!

Monday, 18th December, 1995

6.45pm: No Sleep till Sheffield: Pulp Go Public (BBC Two)

"Tonight's documentary follows the band on tour, culminating in their triumphant homecoming to Sheffield City Hall"

Despite Britpop now being considered a bit of a dirty word for some, with many of the acts who thrived under that banner now considered whatever the polar opposite of groovy is, 1995 was my Year Zero when it came to buying music. I'd soon learn the difference between Cast and Cabaret Voltaire but in Christmas 1995 all I wanted were albums by Blur, Radiohead and of course Pulp. Jarvis interviewed in a full suit on a rumpled hotel bed is charm incarnate but talks about writing songs from the perspective of his thirty-two years with an almost surprised tone when presented with his new screaming teenage fans. He's definitely a kindly older brother figure even of most of these new supporters don't see it that way. Clips of Cocker guesting on television shows a path not taken as the indisputably funny and personable lead singer could easily have taken a path into presenting. *"I now have an opportunity to make a lot of money,"* says Cocker contemplatively, *"I could present some game show and turn into Tarby 2: This Time Its Personal. There's a great deal of potential for me to become the saddest person of 1996. Nobody is immune."*

Also questioned are his mum and grandma are interviewed and are equally hilarious saying they can't see Jarv as a sex symbol arguing that they prefer Steve McQueen (*"unfortunately he was very small..."*) and Ronald Colman respectively. Sheffield residents will get a kick out of seeing the city frozen in time as Jarvis eulogises his home at the end of the tour. *"The fashions have moved on but the mentality remains"* he says before playing "Mis-Shapes", a song that still sounds a clarion call to every indie kid even if they did leave it off the best of.

Outside the cycle of gigging, Pulp are seen on "Live and Kicking" looking on aghast at fellow guest Gary Glitter who is seen shiftily bopping to "Disco 2000" behind the scenes. An extended edit was shown the following Friday with slightly more talk on their sexy content (*"I'd like to be taken seriously as an artist....and a shag as well"*) but mostly it's their support band the Leigh Bowery "art pop heretics" Minty, who get the chop thanks to the lead singer Nicola Bateman's see through plastic hood costume and lack of anything underneath. They get an understandably muted response from the band's new fans but they represent the gulf that's already begun in 'indie' music which two years on from Suede's "Opening Shot" sees way more money and attention up for grabs. Pulp would eventually run screaming from fame, creating the dark, haunted "This Is Hardcore" in 1998 but this is a brilliant window into a world where what I loved and the country loved were just once the same thing.

Wednesday, 21st December, 1995

8.30pm: Next of Kin (BBC One)

"Andrew is flattered by the attentions of another woman."

A seasonal edition of the comedy with the worst premise of any comedy series I have ever seen. For those with short memories or are just lucky Penelope Keith and William Gaunt starred, as the write up in the Radio Times says, as "grandparents who are saddled with their grandchildren". And why are they saddled with them? Oh that's right...BECAUSE THEIR PARENTS ARE DEAD. Yes, this is a sitcom where a spoiled middle class couple are forced to restructure their lives when their estranged son and his wife (whom they lovely call "Bootface") die in an off-screen car crash. Despite the 'joke' supposedly being that we mock their self-absorbed life of leisure, neither character is written to show an ounce of pity and despite being the general point of the show, the kids are almost constantly missing from scenes. As, for that matter, are jokes. Scenes here seem to drift into each other with kamikaze disinterest and the two plot lines - Keith's character getting to reconnect to her old life through a part-time job in tandem with a spurned Gaunt being propositioned by fellow grandparent - are so poorly realised they may as well be on different channels.

Still if you like stereotype tropes such as precocious kids, molly-coddling teachers, middle-class neighbours, jolly working class staff, glamorous grans and a socially conscious daughter being the target for utter hatred then "Next of Kin" could be the sitcom for you. Or a lobotomy. Three series too! It's so very Tory and middle class whilst Penelope Keith fails to connect to the sympathetic strings that made Margo in "The Good Life" or Audrey in "To The Manor Born" something more than two dimensional stereotypes. Having come from writing the safe but generally fine ITV sitcom "Second Thoughts" and its sequel "Faith In The Future" I don't understand how Gavin Petrie and Jan Etherington missed the mark so much. After this they managed just one final sitcom - 1998's "Duck Patrol" - and that was shit as well.

Friday, 22nd December, 1995

10.10pm: Sean Hughes Is Thirty Somehow (Channel 4)

"Comedian Sean Hughes gives a specially recorded stand-up performance at London's Riverside Studios on his 30th birthday."

Having effectively grown up on screen from winning the Perrier Award for best show in Edinburgh aged just 24 to the hugely fun Garry Shandling-influenced sitcom "Sean's Show", it still makes my heart hurt to imagine him no longer around. Much like his contemporaries Newman and Baddiel his early act was always bedded in pop culture and indie music[35] yet shone through with a charm and personality that made him thoroughly likeable.

Watching Hughes here in full flight is a treat, the sheer exuberance and bouncing from idea to idea is a reminder of why he was rated so highly so quickly. He talks about a number of then-recent news items such as the OJ Simpson trial, Snoop Dogg (*"Scooby's mate"*), how quickly people stopped caring about the war in Bosnia and Fred West but only in comparison to his own lack of capability to get women back to his own house. With him no longer here, a section on health is now a tough watch as he talks about smoking and drinking whilst smoking and drinking (*"All the other kids were smoking behind the bike sheds, I was cycling behind the tobacconists"*) There's strong material about parents (*"Has anyone heard their parents making love? I know. You hire out a video and that's the last thing you expect..."*), relationships *("Don't think of it as losing a daughter but gaining a SEX MACHINE....")* and a surprisingly vehement rally

---

[35] Carter USM would provide the theme tune to his BBC Two travelogue series "Sean's Shorts"

about how crap cats are. Hughes' career seemed to slow down around this point with his increasingly-reduced part on "Never Mind The Buzzcocks" his main paycheck from 1996 to 2002. When he died many said it was a great loss which is incredibly true for someone just 51 years old and yet, looking back at all the remarkable things he had done, it was hard not to see it as a life somehow solidly lived.

Sunday, 24th December, 1995

12.35pm: A Flintstone Family Christmas (BBC One)

"Festive pre-historic fun."

Good old Yuletide specials set before the whole Christ bit of Christmas. Despite having been somewhat of a disaster since leaving prime-time for increasingly bad kid-friendly series where they for no reason became cops, kids and adjacent to whatever a Shmoo was. With the live-action tedium of big screen "The Flintstones" fresh in people's minds you'd be forgiven for expecting very little here and yet it's a surprisingly adult and thoughtful half hour. The story starts with Fred and Barney doing errands before a vicious mugger takes their valuables. This turns out to be Stoney a "caveless" child on the streets of Bedrock. As its Christ's birthday week, the Flintstones take him in and with Pebbles (voiced by future comedy goddess Megan Mullally) now an adult he is invited to become one of the family. It's a reboot clearly influenced by the success of "The Simpsons" whilst harking back to its original prime-time sitcom audience. There's still plenty of the old school to enjoy with this and it's good to hear the original voice of Wilma Flintstone, Jean Vander Pyl, in the cast but this is easily the most beautiful the modern stone age family have looked in a long time. The special was nominated for an Emmy - the only time a Flintstones episode has ever been up for the award to date.

And to celebrate all this success Hanna-Barbera returned with "A Flintstones Christmas Carol" the following year…which completely undid the events of "A Flintstone Family Christmas" with Stoney now gone and the Pebbles and Bamm-Bamm characters back to being babies. Yabba Dabba Piss.

Sunday, 24th December, 1995

4.25pm: The Adventures of Mole (Channel 4)

"A. Mole is fed up with all the bustle of spring and sets out for an adventure with Rat and Toad."

There's a lot to recommend this short animation based on Kenneth Grahame's eternally beloved "The Wind in the Willows" including the cast featuring the voices of Peter Davison as Mole, Richard Briers as Rat, Paul Eddington as Badger and Hugh Laurie's turbo-charged Bertie Wooster take on Toad. There's also some gorgeous music with a title theme written by Neil Innes and sung by Kirsty MacColl, plus further music from Midge Ure, Paul Weller and Neil Finn. And yet watching it makes me feel like I'm cheating on Cosgrove Hall's definitive take on Grahame's stories which had run on ITV from 1983 to 1990.

Weirder still, ITV's own big programme for the following day was yet another adaptation of "The Wind in the Willows" which mixed animation and live action plus a similarly high calibre cast with Alan Bennett as Mole, Michael Palin as Ratty, Michael Gambon and Badger and Rik Mayall giving it his all as Mr Toad, as well as Vanessa Redgrave as the narrator. It too is a well-made, beautiful and easy going take on the river bank tales but still not enough to knock out the memory of that earlier stop motion favourite. To confuse things further, yet another version featuring a Monty Python touch would appear in cinemas in late 1996 with Terry Jones' live-action film which he would direct, write and star in accompanied by Eric Idle, Steve Coogan and the cream of British comic talent including Stephen Fry, Victoria Wood and some blokes named John Cleese and Michael Palin. Sadly, none of them contained a toad elevating moment…

Sunday, 24th December, 1995

8.45pm: The Mrs Merton Show (BBC Two)

"Mrs Merton presents her very own Christmas show."

Another comic star it's impossible to imagine no longer being here, Caroline Aherne - at this point still married to New Order's miserable bassist Peter Hook - was always going to be a superstar although it took a while to find the format to suit. Before she was a lightning quick interviewer of unsuspecting celebrities, Mrs Merton had first appeared as one of the few characters from Frank Sidebottom's "Radio Timperley" broadcasts not voiced by Chris Sievey. Both were regulars on Piccadilly Radio in Manchester so it seemed inevitable she'd get sucked into the world of the big headed banjolele boy with an appearance on his debut double album "5:9:88"[36] and later his late night Yorkshire TV series "Frank Sidebottom's Fantastic Shed Show".

Yorkshire would also pilot a similar night time series for Aherne herself in 1991 titled "Mrs Murton's Nightcap". Quite similar to the BBC series that followed, Mrs 'Murton' offers general handy hints and agony aunt advice before interviewing an extremely shy Viz editor Chris Donald (*"you look so young to be so fertile!", "would you like to be the editor of a proper magazine one day?"*) and the Kershaw siblings Liz and Andy (*"Do you remember the Clearasil advert you were in?"*) of whom both opinions are had. It's funny enough[37] and Aherne is great through but crucially misses the audience which would become as much of a character itself in the BBC shows.

Having aged up the character a little and gone back to the original spelling of the surname, Granada would film another pilot "That Nice Mrs Merton" before a series of "The Mrs Merton Show" appeared on BBC Two's post-pub schedules in a gap usually filled by "Fantasy Football League". Despite the late slot, a positive reaction would lead to a quick 7pm repeat run two months later

---

[36] A brilliant running joke features Mrs Merton's baby as Little Frank takes 50p for babysitting when she pops to Altrincham. When his mum's magazines "Woman's Hat Weekly" and "Ladies Blouse Weekly" are no use, Frank attempts to shush baby Reginald with a can of shandy and a Victory V lozenge. Eventually the baby escapes through a hole in Frank's shed so they attempt to pass off Little Frank as him not knowing he's already returned home "drunk out of his mind" on Shandy.

[37] The script is credited to Aherne with radio legend Martin Kelner on whose shows Mrs Merton had been a regular.

and when the second series came round it was nestled at the more presentable 9:30pm on Sunday. This Christmas special found chef Gary Rhodes (*"Do you know whose bowels are made of steel? Judith Chalmers!"*), Johnny Briggs and Amanda Barrie flogging the strange "Coronation Street" album with a cover of "Somethin' Stupid", plus a mildly combative Glenys Kinnock on her sofa. There's a bit too much going on and a sad Christmas song from Merton to a supposed orphan boy doesn't seem to have much a payoff. It's still a delight to revisit with some great jokes from Caroline plus her co-writers Craig Cash, Henry Normal and Dave Gorman, especially when guests attempt to outfox her.

After this the character would return for a new episode in exactly a year but now on BBC One where she'd stay for two further series, the latter a compromise for letting Aherne write a sitcom with Cash. And despite the pleasingly odd follow up "Mrs Merton & Malcolm" not being the expected success many assumed, their other idea about a regular family watching TV proved to be much more popular in the long run.

Monday, 25th December, 1995

12.30pm: Christian Rave Special (Channel 4)

"For many young people, Christian raves are part of regular worship. Christian raves are part of regular worship."

A different kind of Christmas Service courtesy of "God In The House" with a smart waistcoat-wearing young man named Adam Buxton. He introduces us to three different kinds of "raves" starting with the Christian dance act World Wide Message Tribe playing in a real church in Cheadle. The songs all sound pretty much like contemporary dance of the time with break beats and repetitive lyrics, only now with a holy feel. It's pretty much all music (one number is a bit of a sexy slow jam but you know... about Jesus) with pauses for teens to talk about Christ. With up to 500 in the pews, it was clearly finding the audience it aimed at with ten albums and even a minor Billboard dance hit in the States. Backstage they insist they're not a cult to a nodding Buxton who looks a million miles away from the beardy bloke who'd bring us Boggins, Bobo, Blinda Data and BaaadDad.

Next he pops over to a youth church service in a Bournemouth nightclub called Bliss. This is more hip hop and praise with a proper full band – even if the talks by leader Johnny Sertin are a bit school-like with the young types sat cross-legged around him.[38] Finally we're taken to "the Late Late Service" at Woodlands Methodist Church in Glasgow which definitely seems the most fun with lots of dancing and singing plus big video screens. Oh and candles. Lots and lots of candles.

The YouTube upload of this says "must be a spoof?" It isn't but it's definitely hard to tell which side producers World of Wonder were on. Parts feel "give 'em enough rope" as teens read excruciating poems and preach but it's also on us to decide whether we take the earnest messages as positive or something to sneer at. And however you look it's still a lot more fun than "Highway".

---

[38] Sadly for those who might be interested in a session it seems Bliss shut at the start of the last decade. Johnny is still doing the Lord's work at Earlsfield Friary near London and on Twitter.

Monday, 25th December, 1995

7.30pm: Robson & Jerome Christmas Special (ITV)

"Robson and Jerome look back over an extraordinary year."

Retrospectives of the era now hold aloft the likes of Pulp, Oasis and Blur as the sound of summer 1995 and yet one duo easily outsold the alternative crowd and the pop juggernauts that year with two of the three biggest selling singles plus the top selling album to boot. And all they did it with some of the dullest cover versions ever recorded by human mouths. Step forward Robson Green and Jerome Flynn. Best known as actors in the popular 90s drama "Soldier Soldier", the duo had been required to sing "Unchained Melody" to fill for a no-show wedding turn as part of a plotline. Viewers in their thousands apparently contacted ITV to find out how to buy this non-existent single which gave snake-oil salesman Simon Cowell the idea to record the pair singing both that song and, to tie in with the upcoming VE Day anniversary celebrations and soak up those World War II nostalgia quids, "The White Cliffs of Dover". It would stay at Number One for seven weeks. And six months later they'd do it again as the "I Believe"/ "Up on the Roof" double A-side stayed at the top for a month, holding "Wonderwall" in second place to the chagrin of many a parka-hooded indie fan.

To remind people where they'd come from, ITV quickly put together this show although sadly it wasn't the glorious light entertainment shiny floor spectacular with the pair stepping out of a giant R and J and duetting with Barbara Dickson it could've been but more like a slightly more middle-aged version of the BBC teen music magazine "The O Zone" with the chart-topping mates generally pottering about and chatting about their admittedly ridiculous year. It's hard to argue with the power of television here which created a perfectly-targeted, elderly relative seeking missile of inoffensive pop and, rather depressingly, would become the key weapon in chart sales the following decade, once again overseen by the Svengali of shite, Simon Cowell. But not before the Woolpackers and "Teletubbies Say Eh Oh" had been unleashed upon the world. In 2008, producer Mike Stock admitted that the vocals on the record were "assisted" by uncredited session singers but considering most of the copies sold were in landfill or Oxfam, nobody was particularly bothered...

Tuesday 26th December, 1995

7.00pm: Christmas in Emmerdale (ITV)

"The village turns out when the Woolpack and the Malt Shovel face each other in a tug of war."

Despite being a regular sight on British TV since 1972 this was the Dale's first appearance on Boxing Day. Forever a bit of a punch line and the poor cousin to "Coronation Street", the rural Yorkshire soap had been on a mission to become vaguely relevant in the 90s since shedding the "Farm" part of its title in 1989. A new production team would expand the focus of the series to the nearby village and then, just for good value, dropped a plane on it. Not a turn of phrase but a real, actual plane. The crash landing on December 30th 1993 allowed producers to completely reshape the series at the same time as getting the attention of audiences who had previously dismissed it (fairly) as a boring countryside affair.

Since 1997, "Emmerdale" has been part of the Christmas Day schedule every year and has so far managed four marriages, three murders, two births and one mineshaft trapping amongst the wacky adventures that happened over the holiday period. Oh and if you're on tender-hooks or had a bet on, the Woolpack won the tug of war competition against the Malt Shovel. Good job that there Hunter from "Gladiators" just happened to be passing, eh?

Pah, and they say soaps aren't realistic…

Thursday, 28th December, 1995

10.20pm: They Think It's All Over (BBC One)

"A festive version of the comedy sports quiz with special guests: comedian Mel Smith and Test cricketer Allan Lamb."

Despite its infamous blindfolded sportsperson groping round being the only vaguely memorable thing about it, "They Think It's All Over" managed three appearances on Christmas Day itself despite being rarely suited to the festive period in the slightest. Originally a Radio 5 programme hosted by Des Lynam and featuring Rory Bremner and Rory McGrath as team captains this had been quickly piloted for TV before Lynam decided it wasn't for him. The series proper would see Bremner cut in favour of sports-based personalities - cricketer David Gower and a newly-retired Gary Lineker – whilst McGrath would hang on as a regular second banana, joined by Lee Hurst. The host was the sharp and football-mad Nick Hancock who had impressed with another Radio 5 to telly transfer "Room 101" the previous year.

With football becoming fashionable again with Nick Hornby's "Fever Pitch", the launch of the glossy "FourFourTwo" and Baddiel and Skinner's "Fantasy Football League", it seemed a good time to launch a quiz named after one of the most famous commentator quotes of all time. As for the humour, time has probably not been kind to the schoolboy sniggering but seeing people known for being strait-laced like original captain Gary Lineker being encouraged into doing something rude could be greatly enjoyable. Although Lee Hurst definitely seemed a much better idea at the time.

Monday, 1st January, 1996

4.50pm: Coastermania (BBC Two)

"In this study, on-board cameras capture the white-knuckle appeal of the rides and fanatics discuss their devotion."

An enjoyable BBC Wales documentary featuring a quality brand of eccentric in the mix of British and American rollercoaster fans interviewed here. There's Reverend Nick Bralesford who asked his wife to marry him on Blackpool's Big Dipper ride. Both go on an US coaster-based road trip wearing their matching "No Rollercoasters in Hell" shirts and listening to the audio book of the New Testament… twice. Another Reverend in the US specialises performing marriage ceremonies on rollercoasters. Long-suffering partners look on in loving bemusement with one in particular Tina Hine struggling to hide her frustration about the lack of non-rollercoaster based outings in her life. Her partner Andy is the founder of the Roller Coaster Club of Great Britain who are later seen making a pilgrimage to Cedar Point Ohio chanting coaster stats and singing "Agadoo". But its harmless fun and they're clearly having a whale of a time with one member helpfully offering the riding advice "wear a jockstrap as it's a bit painful". There's some interesting history of rollercoasters and one fan moots that the developments in the world of amusement rides reflect the overall technological leaps of the world. On the other side of that are traditional wooden rollercoasters debated by some interviewees as real art, something that's hard to deny when we see the construction from scratch of what will become Megafobia in Wales. There's also the wooden Phoenix at a Pennsylvania amusement resort run by a chap named Dick Knoebel which is not funny and shame on you for laughing at it.

As a regular visitor to Blackpool in the 80s and 90s it's lovely to see shots of how it used to be with the brand new Pepsi Max Big One looming large above. There's also the American equivalent in the slightly shabby, well-worn Coney Island and various exciting Japanese equivalents that look absolutely terrifying.

Generally the tone is upbeat throughout and it seems that the love never really dies as in 2020 the Phoenix remains one of the most beloved wooden rides in the world, the Roller Coaster Club of GB are still going strong and Andy Hine even received an MBE from The Queen for "uniting people and promoting tourism".

1996

Highest Rated Programme: How could it be anything other than "Only Fools and Horses" with 24 million tuning in on the 29th December for "Time On Our Hands" making it the fifth most watched UK programme of all time. On Christmas Day itself the Trotters also scooped the top spot with an especially depressing episode of Corrie involving Don Brennan trying to top himself and a Des O'Connor special being the only ITV representation in a comedy-heavy top ten.

Big Films on the BBC: Willy is freed on Boxing Day in 1993's "Free Willy" and it's Firm. Sorry, that should've read 'it's joined by "The Firm" with Tom Cruise' which is also on. Really though it's all about "Jurassic Park" on Christmas Day which despite everyone in the world seeing it at the time still did deservedly huge business for the Beeb with 14 and a half million dinofans watching throughout. Sadly it wasn't The Director's Cut, with extra dinosaurs. Classics were ahoy on BBC Two with "The Producers", "Casablanca", "Easter Parade", "The Italian Job", "Singin' In The Rain", "Brief Encounter" and "Angels With Dirty Faces" just a few of the films on offer. Premieres include "Glengarry Glen Ross", Oliver Stone's "Heaven and Earth", the micro-budget action of Robert Rodriguez's "El Mariachi", behemoth Altman work "Short Cuts" and the grim comic artist documentary "Crumb" which I saw in the midst of a raging fever and felt like a distressing dream at points.

Big Films on ITV: A bit of class for once with "The Remains of the Day", "The Secret Garden", Hitchcock's "Topaz" and "A Man For All Seasons" amongst the offerings although the less said about 'incorrect TV menace' "Dennis" on Christmas Day the better. Devotees of Christmas film "Die Hard" will also be pleased to know its scheduled…on New Year's Day. Ho Ho…huh?

Big Films on Channel 4: The delightful but deeply unsuccessful "Toys" is on surprisingly late at 9pm as is the more famous of the Christopher Columbus biopics - the ridiculously long "1492: Conquest of Paradise". And for those up at 2:50am on Boxing Day night there's Bob Hoskins' directorial debut "The Raggedy Rawney" which I'd previously assumed was just something Adam & Joe made up for their "Bobo!" song.

Oh That Queen's Speech: Nelson Mandela popped over for a visit so everyone looked busy and tried not to sing The Special AKA. Jacques Chirac came too but he didn't have a 1984 hit single written about him so no-one cared. She didn't find space to mention Gazza's cheeky dummy into a storming goal in the 79th minute against Scotland in Euro '96 but her bicep tattoo of Teddy Sheringham was particularly well done.

For The Kids: Take your pick! BBC One has four hours of mulch including the animated "The Legend of Prince Valiant", teen bollocks "Sweet Valley High" and manic game show "Incredible Games". Channel 4 score best with a decent line up of sitcom "Hangin' With Mr Cooper", "The Crystal Maze" and the decent "Back To The Future" spin-off animated series. But the biggest news is that "He-Man" has finally gone from ITV – replaced by "Captain Simian and the Space Monkeys" and "Santo Bugito" followed by Patrick Duffy and Suzanne Somers in the most average American family sitcom "Step by Step". BBC One also used this period to burn off episodes of "Muppets Tonight" after it hadn't performed well in prime-time even though it was great fun and people are idiots.

The Pops: Taking a cue from 1994's casting of the year's biggest pop act as hosts, it came as little surprise that the still ten-legged groove phenomenon that was the Spice Girls introduced this year's edition of "Top of the Pops". It was a year of two halves with the disparate likes of Babylon Zoo, Robert Miles, The Prodigy and the Manic Street Preachers all having equal success before pop was brought screaming back to the fore by two Melanies, a Geri, Emma and Victoria who give us a bit of "Wannabe" AND "Say You'll Be There". There's also room for a newly single Robbie Williams, The Fugees, Gina G and a rare sighting of Babybird in the mix which is generally agreeable for all. Over on ITV that night Des O'Connor had those titans of pop Diana Ross, Julio Iglasias and, um… The Woolpackers.

Radio Times Cover: A jovial snowman in a newly unwrapped jack in a box tips his hat cheerfully with the right hand yet holds a rolled up copy of that self-same £1.50 Radio Times slightly menacingly. And lower those eyebrows, chum! As for the movie situation, there are 800....PLUS! Granted that might be 801 but that is an addition sign well earned!

TV Times Cover: A change of pace from gurning Santas as a gurning Wallace and Gromit wish the audience a "Cracking Christmas" despite not having any new adventures scheduled. But the economy is clearly on the rise as we're back up to 18 cars for the winning! And still £1.20!

New Year's Daze: More sideways looks at the year from Angus Deayton at 11pm on BBC One with "Hogmanay Live" now thankfully free of sex offenders. And it's all rockin' and slash or rollin' on Two with two specials from 1968 – "The Rolling Stones' Rock and Roll Circus" and "Elvis – the 68 Comeback Special" either side of Jools who has Elton, Weller and…sigh, Hucknall. Still, The Lighthouse Family will calm our jangled nerves. Over on ITV, a quick trip to Trevor McDonald to see the New Year around a showing of the dismal Eddie Murphy vehicle "The Golden Child" alongside Channel 4 taking several visits to Birmingham City Hospital for live coverage of how they cope over New Year's Eve with Dr Phil Hammond and the Dad from "My Parents Are Aliens".

Theme Nights: Natural History Night is the flimsy pretence on the 28th December for BBC Two to bang out a load of wildlife repeats including a 1976 "The World About Us" about the Namib desert, "Kingdom of the Ice Bear" and best of all, "On The Tracks of The Wild Otter" from 1982. Because otters. Naturally, Attenborough presides throughout.

Wouldn't Happen Now: ITV had "Christmas with the Royal Navy", a series of five live programmes throughout Christmas Day hosted from HMS Belfast by Anthea Turner. No doubt a wonderful service for naval officers and their loved ones the rest of us were expected to entertain ourselves by looking at…boats?

New For '97: Frank Skinner's chat show is back as is "Big Break" and "Emmerdale" goes thrice weekly. Chris Morris' "Brass Eye" finally got on air in late January after several delays but all the big money's really on Channel 4's other new comedy that month - the new Craig Charles pirate themed sitcom called "Captain Butler". It's gonna be bigger than Smeg Outs!!!! There's also the matter of the UK's fifth terrestrial channel launching that March….

Is The Sound Of Music On? No! I'm beginning to think I should've picked "Gone With The Wind" instead…

Saturday, 21st December, 1996

5.35pm: The Simpsons (BBC One)

"Seasonal satire with the Simpsons."

When the BBC first got the rights to show episodes of "The Simpsons" in 1996 a lot of commentators and fans wondered what the point was. Firstly they had already been responsible for cutting out the short early appearances by the family in "The Tracey Ullman Show" when it appeared on BBC Two in order to squeeze it into a 20 minute timeslot. But more importantly the animated sitcom was now onto its eighth season and Sky One, where it had been airing since 1990, were barely weeks behind the American showings. And this was a series that had refined and improved upon itself constantly, long outstripping its initial burst of popularity with the hit singles, acres of merchandise and video games that appeared between 1990 and 1991. There had also been a series of top-selling videos featuring the frankly underwhelming early episodes BBC were going to be stuck with when launching "The Simpsons" as part of their big Saturday night schedule. Despite going on to show a mix of episodes from the first three seasons seemingly at random it made no difference and the ratings were horrible, being beaten every week by another import on ITV - "Sabrina The Teenage Witch".

BBC One eventually handed it over to BBC Two where it took off in the much lower-pressure 6pm teatime slot where it would happily remain until Channel 4 swiped it in 2004[39]. By far the most important programme of the nineties, it's strange that it hasn't really come up much in this book yet due to this episode "Simpsons Roasting On An Open Fire" - the first to be broadcast in the US after the season was delayed due to initial animation coming back barely useable - being the only Christmas themed special until season 7's magnificent "Marge Be Not Proud" which wouldn't make it to terrestrial TV until September 2000.

Saturday, 21st December, 1996

7.00pm: Noel's....and the Winner Is (BBC One)

"Noel Edmonds presents an award ceremony with a difference."

Time to check in with Noel again four years after his "House Party" was hitting its peak and we're presented with a new format...if you can even call it a format. The clumsily-titled "Noel's And The Winner Is..." takes the form of a black tie awards ceremony for lots of daft real hobbies and activities. But it's also got sketches in it. Oh, and a quiz at the end. Most of which doesn't conform to the basic premise of "winning" but I'm getting ahead of myself...

We open on a lit up TV Centre just so you feel nice and miserable about it being turned into flats before Noel comes on to do some topical gags including one about the Cantona Kick which had

---

[39] "The Simpsons" would eventually return to BBC One briefly as part of the dreadful Emma Ledden and Steve Wilson era of "Live and Kicking" despite it neither being a kids series or in any way suitable.

occurred nearly two years earlier. Next we see clips of a Gut Barging Contest, a Lithuanian Kissing Marathon, the Toe Wrestling Championships in Derbyshire and Rear of the Year[40]. Apparently there's a winner from all these and the Lithuanians win and so to collect their prize here's....um, Louise "Not Yet Redknapp" Nurding who reads a statement supposedly written by them featuring some jokes about Chapstick and Lipsyl. Noel makes a clumsy joke about kissing her despite a 26 year age gap and a nation outwardly winces.

Next is a dreadful sketch where Noel supposedly talks to "Pricilla Precious live from Hollywood" on a satellite link with comedy time delay responses ripped off that "Two Ronnies" Mastermind sketch meaning she answers the questions out of sync which ends up sounding A BIT RUDE. The routine comes in under 90 seconds and has nothing to do with "winning" but that's just another factor contributing to this strange FrankenNoel's Monster of a show with its weird, tacky atmosphere and 'funny foreigners' clips making it not dissimilar to a sexless episode of "Eurotrash". In case your neck wasn't broken enough from the mood whiplash, there's room for a sad dog story then we greet the World Snail Racing Champion, a pre-teen who looks terrified to be there, especially when joined by a hollering John McCririck. The very darkest recesses of the barrel are discovered however when we're promised the arrival from "Kermit the Frog" only to get a green sock puppet being voiced by Bobby Davro. It was at this point I

[40] That year's victor was Coronation Street's Tracy Shaw who would be the last solo winner. A man would be chosen too from the following year with Melinda Messenger and... Gary Barlow!? the first joint winners. Yay feminism.

looked at the clock and saw there was nearly 25 minutes of the programme left. If I get to the end, do I win something too?

Thankfully the show suddenly pivots into a quiz entitled "Noel's Know All of 96" with celebrity guests Rhona Cameron, Eddie "I Don't Do Television" Izzard and Carol Vorderman answering questions on the year gone by. This feels more on Noel's level and possibly could've been a show of its own but even with material written by Paul Merton's comedy partner John Irwin all of the celebrities involved look like they want to go and have a hard talk with their agents the second it's done.

It's easy to see why Noel was probably looking for something else to host around this point as "House Party" was five years in now and seen as a bit naff post-Mr Blobby, "Telly Addicts" had reached a decade on screen the previous year and its short-lived spin-off "Noel's Telly Years" wasn't really grabbing anyone. But this was an ugly mess of half thought out ideas which is a shame as the "daft contests" segments probably would've worked as a five minute weekly slot on "House Party". Mercifully, despite being a show all about winners, this was a definite loser heading toward the nearest canal with a brick in a sack.

Saturday, 21st December, 1996

8.50pm: Gogs (BBC Two)

"The story of Stone-Age folk."

Following in the footprints of Wallace and Gromit, here was an all-new Claymation series… assuming you ignore it already airing on Welsh language channel S4C in 1993. These short five-minute dialogue free tales of some socially incapable cavemen were stripped over Christmas 1996 in seemingly random time slots anywhere between 3pm and 11:15pm. Despite the moving target somebody must've found it and more episodes followed with the thirty-minute finale Gogwana going out on Christmas Day 1998.[41] It's well made and won lots of acclaim but also one of the ugliest things I have ever seen and manages to be visually repellent and yet boring simultaneously. I can appreciate the craft that went into the animation but it comes over as just gross and more than a little bit creepy with lots of Looney Tunes style eye-popping big screaming faces and jokes almost solidly about bottoms or poo. Now I love a good bum gag - just ask my doctor - but it's wearing and relentless to the point of tedium here. I'm going to have the Gog Council on my back now, aren't I?

Sunday, 22nd December, 1996

8.00pm: Autobahn Blues (Channel 4)

"Legendary DJ John Peel sets off on a journey around Germany in his trusty Mercedes 190."

When John Peel died in 2004 I, like millions of others, was heartbroken. His was a style and a tone which was unique and impossible to replicate with a passion for the things he loved

---

[41] A similar cramming of animation into every Christmas slot available would happen again in 1998 with the brilliant "Rex the Runt" in 1998 and adventure spoof "The Big Knights" in 1999.

above all of this contemporaries. And yet if I'm really honest it was never his Radio 1 shows that I was a dedicated fan of but his speech radio work like "Home Truths" - a Saturday morning Radio 4 compendium of listeners' anecdotes. Some were sad, many were hilarious but with Peel at the helm it always felt like an accessible lively show and he constantly seemed sincerely interested in the people he spoke to. This edition of Channel 4's homemade travelogue series "Travels with My Camera" finds him very much in that latter role.

Beginning with a sketchy idea of where to head and a broken toe, John sets off to Hamburg (*"To some people Hamburg means the Beatles and not much more...Liverpool has a similar problem..."*) to meet the people behind some of the community stations he has been providing pre-recorded programmes for starting with FSK - a sponsor-run micro-broadcaster - who interview him in their tiny studios (*"At least you won't bump into Chris Evans here!"*) He monologues that people seeing with a camera crew will assume he's the star of a gritty detective series as he heads to a tunnel under the river Elbe which reminds him of the Mersey tunnel and he rightly points out would look amazing in a pop video[42].

Taught to hate Germans at birth due to the war in Europe, Peel's is not an attitude of anything other than optimistic discovery which equates to humans and places as much as the noisy bits of vinyl which history seems determined to pigeonhole him as playing. Not that music is far from this documentary and he seems at his happiest when filmed going wild in a record store picking up

---

[42] Apparently Scooter later did this but they don't count because they're Scooter and also shut up Sarah.

titles (*"you always look to see if it's got a keyboard player on it and if there is you don't buy it..."*) because of their strange names or obscure labels. Looking in a tattooist's window he considers getting one himself to frighten his family, perhaps featuring *"the repeal of the Corn Laws on my manly thighs"*.

Duisburg follows before we're met by a different FSK - this one is the band who regular listeners to Peel's music shows will be very familiar with – holed up in an ex-police drunk tank in Munich playing incredible music pitched somewhere between indie and folk yet sounding like neither. Over to the former East Germany for a walk round the former Colditz which most local Germans have never even heard of or knew the mythic nature of (*"can you name a British prisoner of war camp? Neither can I."*) Less than a decade since re-unification, he speaks to fans about the window into a different world his broadcasts provided and how difficult it was to find punk records in socialist state. The art and architecture of that era still remains and provides a window to a place we can never truly imagine life within from the outside. He's brutally honest whether talking about sex, his relationship with his reserved father and his relationship with fame (*"Are you who we think you are? How am I supposed to answer that!")* There's also a lot of stock put on the individualism of Europe that he predicts, sadly with keen accuracy, would slowly become an amorphous whole without character. As such it's good to have this funny, fascinating record permanently captured. Indeed the only real downside is that Channel 4 didn't send Peel all over the world to record similar shows like a post-punk Palin. Prost!

Monday, 23rd December, 1996

6.30pm: The Brittas Empire (BBC One)

"Brittas organises a special Christmas treat for his staff. It's a team-bonding exercise in the Welsh mountains."

One of the BBC's biggest sitcoms of the 90s yet rarely ever mentioned since, "The Brittas Empire" was on the surface a show about a leisure centre with an incompetent manager but, much like its contemporary "2 Point 4 Children", a surreal, almost savage streak ran throughout. If Gordon Brittas made it out of each series without being injured, bruised or even killed he was onto a winner. And audiences lapped it up due to him being so naively dreadful that he could only be played by Chris Barrie, a man with experience in making awful people acceptable and even a bit lovable. That was also partly achieved by surrounding him with a cast of equally neurotic, broken characters such as the emotional receptionist Carole (Harriet Thorpe) who often would have her young children hidden around the leisure centre, his highly-strung wife Helen (Pippa Haywood) and jealous pool manager Tim (Russell Porter) whose same-sex relationship with the more stable Gavin (Tim Marriott) was still unique for a family sitcom. The only sane person is deputy manager Laura (Julia St John) though the medically unfortunate handyman Colin (Michael Burns) is happily oblivious to his repulsive nature.

Throughout five series, Gordon was attacked by a JCB, electrocuted, shot at, had his brakes cut, had his feet set in concrete, was caught in an explosion and crushed by a water tank saving Carole. This last act was how the series was supposed to conclude with creators Fegen & Norriss deciding to send him off in a noble, glorious fashion. [43]

The BBC weren't as keen to give up on a hit series however and so a further sixteen episodes were produced by a team of writers with Gordon shown being sent back to Earth by Saint Peter who has been driven insane by his behaviour. "Surviving Christmas" by Tony Millan and Mike Walling came just before the seventh series which would finally close the book on the staff of Whitbury Newtown Leisure Centre. This 1996 special[44] finds Brittas typically driving everyone, including the burly ex-SAS instructor (Mark Arden) teaching the course, insane along with his wife who believes he's having an affair ("*Sorry about that. I'm afraid my wife's a woman*!") due to one of those sitcom style misunderstandings. It quickly becomes clear that someone is watching them and sends several violent messages to prove it. Naturally, Brittas is oblivious and it only gets worse from there...

Over surprisingly quickly, it's a strange mix of farce and slapstick but misses the genuine surrealism of earlier episodes. It's also missing Julia St John who left after the fifth series and whose character was largely the more fleshed out, recognisably normal

---

[43] Confusing matters the episode immediately following that - the series' first Christmas special from 1994 - shows a very much alive Gordon at the end of a flash-forward episode set in the distant moon year of 2019.

[44] The same year, the whole cast would also appear as part of the Royal Variety Performance inspecting the auditorium. It's a very funny little three minute sketch about European rules leading to strange time zones ("*The people on that side of the line have already seen the show...and you people haven't even arrived...*")

core of "The Brittas Empire" allowing the more cartoonish characters to run riot. It was around this time that Chris Barrie would state he was sick of playing losers and after controversially leaving midway through series seven of "Red Dwarf" began a new BBC One sitcom by the authors of this "Brittas" episode titled "A Prince Amongst Men" about a cocky ex footballing star which was so calamitous it was eventually shifted to Sunday afternoons. Presumably to give all the other programmes a chance.

Monday, 23rd December, 1996

11.25pm: In the Dark with Julian Clary (ITV)

"Julian Clary challenges three couples to take on crazy challenges in total darkness as they compete for a star prize."

A very late slot for a big entertainment pilot with a noted star? Nothing suspicious there. Nope. This is the latest vehicle for the brilliant but hard to programme for Julian Clary who always works best just riffing off members of the public. There are some here but sadly there's a high concept game-show attached involving couples trying to find things…in the dark. Do you see? The title! The game! It works on so many levels!

From the second Clary walks onto a Day-Glo house set looking like it's been pinched from CITV he's up against it. Despite some on-point innuendo and an all too brief bit of fun with the audience (when the studio is pitch black, he tells them to imagine spiders falling on their heads to huge chaos and genuine laughter), the contestants are dull and it doesn't get better when it's time to play the game which is effectively a naughty version of children's' programme "Finders Keepers" with added night vision cameras plus the chance that someone might touch another person accidentally on the bosoms and / or penis.

Despite one of the producers of "Don't Forget Your Toothbrush" being involved, the ideas fall flat and the joke has worn pretty thin by the end of part one. Which is why it's particularly strange that the format sold all over the world including the newly-formed WB network in the United States who hired Clary for a full prime-time series which he duly filmed and then saw pulled from the schedule six hours before the first broadcast due to it not being "up to the standards we had for this network..." claimed CEO Jamie Kellner in a 1997 interview. You can see why they wanted the original host as "In The Dark" would be nothing with Clary and indeed, after this pilot, it wasn't as Channel 5 bought the format as a post-pub vehicle for pleasant but uninteresting Junior Simpson.

Tuesday, 24th December, 1996

10.00pm: Father Ted Christmas Special (Channel 4)

"It should be a heavenly time for Father Ted..."

The newspaper Metro once printed ten reasons why "A Christmassy Ted" is the greatest Christmas TV special ever. Of course they were wrong as it's overlong, baggy and has three plots that don't really ever converge to a satisfying whole. And yet it's still one of the funniest Christmas comedies of the past 25 years. Considering how ubiquitous it still is on TV I probably don't need to explain the plot – or plots – to you but the bit that most people remember is Ted leading a party of perplexed priests out of "Ireland's biggest lingerie section". The second half where he wins a Golden Cleric Award for the above before a conman tries to steal it after the awards ceremony (which is for some reason on Christmas Day) is perhaps less memorable yet it's still full of great lines, not to mention the sight of guest star Gerard McSorley shadow boxing in his underpants (*"Well, here we are now, all the lads..."*) as the mysterious Father Todd Unctious.

Despite the fact none of the storylines really fit together there are so many sight gags (Dougal covered in glitter and stickers, poor old Larry Duff making is final appearance), quotable lines (*"He gives good mass…", "Ruud Gullit sitting on a shed", "You let Dougal do a funeral!??", "Father Peter Perfect, the Perfect Priest", "he should be under 'Liars' rather than 'Twats'..."*), throwaway bits (Priest Chatback with a cameo from a young Ed Byrne in particular is glorious) and smaller running threads such as Mrs Doyle's battle with an insensitively purchased tea-making machine that it flies by at enough speed that it doesn't really matter.

After a slow start to the first series[45] "Father Ted" had really taken off during its ten-episode second run which remains consistently great from "small…far away" to "What am I doing on the fecking wheel?!" Having already written so much in 1996, writers Arthur Mathews and the other one decided a Christmas special would buy them some time before needing to tackle another full series and yet would describe it as *"infinitely harder to write than any episode"* in

[45] Which premiered on Channel 4 the same day – 21st April 1995 - as some import programme called "Friends".

the series' 1999 script book, Mathews suggesting that *"perhaps Craggy Island is too mad and too surreal to handle an hour of comedy".*

One of the last truly brilliant British sitcoms, it would return for a final series in 1998 which would finish filming the day before lead actor Dermot Morgan passed away aged just 45. As epitaphs go, "A Christmassy Ted" cropping up every year will ensure his brilliant work is seen for generations to come yet.

Wednesday, 25th December, 1996

2.30pm: Year In Review - Diana Princess of Wales (Sky One)

"The stories about Diana that made the headlines in 1996"

For those who didn't live through 1997 it's impossible to convey the mix of emotions and reactions to Diana's tragic death that year. Eddie Izzard equated it to showing a final episode of "The X Files" unannounced in the middle of the night and people going "oh I was watching that…" It was an event that the whole world felt, regardless of whether they were upset or not. Before her death, programmes like this were everywhere with constant press stories and communal fascination. And so it was that afterwards when public opinion had turned against the intrusive media that had effectively played a huge part in the crash everything changed and there were never any problems with the tabloid newspapers ever again. Well a boy can dream, cant he?

Thursday, 26th December, 1996

11pm: Man Made News (Paramount Channel)

Despite its low stature and grab bag schedule of old American sitcoms and drama series nobody else fancied, the Paramount (no 'Comedy' - that would come later) Channel invested a lot in new comic talent. Initially employing folk like Simon Pegg, Matt Lucas and David Walliams to produce short sketches to fit around an evening's programming wraparound content for the regular schedules they quickly expanded to full half hours with "Asylum", a very loose sitcom set in a mental asylum allowing supposedly committed comedians, including Julian Barratt, Adam Bloom, Bill Bailey, Paul Tonkinson and Andy Parsons, to do their acts. Directed by Edgar Wright and starring Pegg and Jessica Stevenson, it would become a stepping stone to "Spaced" and all the films that followed. Paramount's first head of programming Myfanwy Moore, who knew Walliams from university and would go on to produce "Little Britain", told Chortle in 2008: *"When we started, talent wasn't going to put up with being on cable and being told what to do. So we gave them a certain amount of artistic freedom."*

Much less memorable was the live Dominik Diamond-hosted "Man Made News" with Rhona Cameron, Sean Lock, Felix Dexter and Kevin Day regulars although it would be its assistant producer Dom Joly who made the biggest impression. Whilst not a success[46], it was a good example of how Paramount was open to experiment with Armstrong and Miller, Sasha Baron-Cohen and

[46] Joly's autobiography claims it averaged 6,000 viewers and he had to provide the phone calls for the live call-in section as nobody was ringing in.

some bloke from the art department called Leigh Francis getting some of their earliest exposure there.

Saturday, 28th December, 1996

12.40pm: Star Trek: 30 Years and Beyond (BBC Two)

"Highlights from a special gala that brought together actors and guest stars from Star Trek to celebrate the popular series."

An edit of a two hour live special from October 1996, "30 Years and Beyond" found the Star Trek franchise at a high as "The Next Generation" cast progressed to the big screen with top-notch "First Contact" still new in cinemas along with "Deep Space Nine" and "Voyager". Indeed, you couldn't move for the bloody stuff on BBC Two at this time with three nights a week featuring something from the world of Gene Roddenberry's world of exciting space adventures. After twenty years of people making jokes about Shatner's acting, wobbly sets and doomed redshirts, the world of "Star Trek" was finally becoming respected again… and so here's a special show to completely kick that up the arse.

Hosted by Ted Danson "live from Hollywood" this is what happens when people who don't understand the popularity of a thing attempt to celebrate it. A great comic actor but no host, Danson stumbles over the word "Bajorans" in his opening line and it doesn't get much better from there. Joan Collins arrives to talk about her 1967 cameo in perhaps the best original series episode "City of the Edge of Forever" but she's easily trumped by Nichelle Nichols, Nyota Uhura in the original "Star Trek", who shares an anecdote about meeting a fan in the sixties named Martin Luther-King. Another fan is the still fairly-obscure Ben Stiller who performs an over-specific stand up spot about the original programme whilst displaying an ignorance to everything else (*"Bones...Sulu...Scotty...I know you have real names that escape me at this moment"*) A second sketch found Kate Mulgrew in a fake "Voyager" screen test with Jane Leeves, Peri Gilpin and David Hyde Pierce from "Frasier". It's a fun if not especially funny piece with John Mahoney playing Captain in his infamous green armchair as Eddie the dog causes trouble with the Klingons. And Kelsey Grammar stays home to probably have some of that famous sex he was always enjoying.

Just as you start to get settled in we're promised an appearance by "one of the finest musicians of our time" – unfortunately this turns out to be the parping, god-awful Kenny G who plays his terrible wine bar music as a sequence of special effects are presented on screen. Only mildly less vom-inspiring is mezzo-soprano opera singer Jennifer Larmore with her interpretation of John Lennon's "Imagine" which apparently paid tribute to "the spirit and humanity of Gene Roddenberry". Still, there's always Buzz Aldrin to remind us that he went TO THE BLOODY MOON, MATE. As for the casts, Shatner's there, Stewart isn't but drops a filmed "hello" in, as does Nimoy who stands in front of the Eiffel Tower as if to provide an alibi for his whereabouts. Most of the others turn up and as they're gathered on stage are awarded miniature American flags that have apparently come from the space station. It's a touching reminder of those many people who boldly went where no man, woman or Ted Danson has been before...

Sunday, 29th December, 1996

3.25pm: Wizard of Oz on Ice (BBC One)

"Bobby McFerrin narrates the tale of Dorothy who is danced by Olympic gold medallist Oksana Baiul and sung by Shanice."

Another sincerely mad bit of US prime-time programming bringing together "Don't Worry Be Happy" star McFerrin as everyone his fellow pop star Shanice didn't play and former British figure skater Robin Cousins who was "special choreographer and creative consultant" here. Despite having turned professional in 1980, the 36 year old Cousins was still winning competitions up to 1992 whilst working on productions like this and would later bring Starlight Express and Toy Story to the icy arena. Despite this British element it feels like the most American thing ever and had originally aired in February of 1996 on US station CBS.

Sunday, 29th December, 1996

8.00pm: Only Fools and Horses (BBC One)

"Raquel is worried…"

How do you find something new to say about "Only Fools and Horses"? It is the programme that, more than any other, the British public have taken to their heart and refused to let go of decades after its initial conclusion. Nearly 25 million people saw this episode go out live - no mean feat in the satellite era - making it the fifth most watched TV programme ever. The clip of Del passing out when he learns how much the pocket watch which had been lying in their garage for years was selling at auction is written into the nation's soul, just next to Del and Rodney dressed as Batman and Robin from the earlier "Heroes and Villains".

However there's surprisingly little mentioned of the sitcom's more dramatic scenes which had increasingly become part of the OFAH's heart since it had stretched to 50 minutes an episode in 1989. This finally allowed creator John Sullivan to push the Trotter brothers' storylines along with realistic relationships, marriages and bar fallings. As well as Del's attempts to better his lot, the running thread throughout these final three episodes is Rodney and Cassandra's attempts for a baby which unexpectedly ends in a tragic miscarriage. Taking place in the second episode "Modern Men" after 45 minutes of daftness about Del considering a vasectomy and Rodney looking for work the news hits like a sucker punch and inspires genuine emotion for these characters that have become so real over the previous 15 years.

As the third and final part of Sullivan's 1996 trilogy of stories begins you can't help wondering how they're going to address this sadness, be it a time jump or just completely ignoring it. For a time, it seems like the latter is going to be the case with Raquel fretting about her parents meeting Del for the first time. The Trotter brothers go to clear out their garage but on the way back find themselves trapped in the grotty lift in Nelson Mandela House. It's here that the episode's real stand out moments occur as a despondent Rodney begins to slowly talk about what happened after bottling it up and drinking it away for weeks. Featuring just David Jason and Nicholas Lyndhurst, this is one of the most powerful scenes from not just any sitcom but TV in general. John Sullivan had already tackled grief superbly when writing the real life death of Lennard Pearce into the fourth series but here the pain is so real because we as a nation have seen Rodney go from pot-smoking shiftless adolescent to a grown married man. He's part of the family. The Rodney plonker. The speech he gives is truthful but devastatingly performed by Lyndhurst who has never been better.

After that it's more or less back to the gags as Raquel's dinner party goes naturally awry before her antiques dealer father spots the watch that would make their fortune. After years of saying it, the Trotters were now actually millionaires. Cue a walk into an animated sunset (*"This time next year we could be billionaires!"*) and a genuine celebratory tear for a series that went from just another sitcom to the series that frequently united the nation. Countless documentaries and clip shows followed with David Jason releasing about 400 books "just remembering" that he was originally asked to play Grandad or Mickey Pearce's hat or the chandelier at some point. A thousand "Nag's Head" pubs popped up in every sunny European location full of ex-pats and truckloads of official tie-in merchandise, every bit as tacky as some of the items Del sold on his market stall, appeared in shops all over the country. It ended on a high with an unrealistic situation that everybody wanted to happen. Everyone went back to their other projects and despite the demands from idiots who don't understand when something is best left alone, John Sullivan promised he would never write another "Only Fools" script….and then of course he wrote three.

Premiering on Christmas Days 2001 through 2003 this new trilogy felt like a cruel joke which needed to return the Trotters to the bottom of the pile for no reason other than the BBC had nothing better to air. Only now they weren't plucky hopeful chancers, they were morons who blew their money and now had to live with the consequences. The jokes were just not as funny this time round and frequently felt recycled from earlier episodes. It only got worse with the Boycie-centric spin-off "The Green Green Grass" which felt like an escapee from the 1970s and the sort of programme "Only Fools and Horses" once felt believably different next to.

With John Sullivan's death in 2011 it seemed people were now finally happy to let Del and Rodney be and at the very least the hunger for it could be sated by switching on to the GOLD channel most hours of the day where it is seemingly in a never ending repeat cycle. There was also the official musical co-written by Paul Whitehouse with Sullivan's son Jim and Chas Hodges of "And Dave" fame which opened to huge acclaim in the West End in 2019. Not a bad little earner, all in all or as Del might say it "Bonnet de douche".

Monday, 30 December, 1996

8.30pm: Changing Rooms (BBC Two)

"Carol Smillie looks back on autumn's series…"

A relatively straight-forward bit of home improvement porn on BBC Two, "Changing Rooms" would quickly become one of the biggest shows on television thanks to a mixture of DIY tips, quirky characters and, above all, the chance that the people whose home was being cheaply renovated predominantly around the concept of style rather than function would absolutely bloody despise what had been done. A shuffle over to BBC One was in store for the third series in 1998 where for some in explicable reason it was given the 6:30pm slot on Christmas Day itself. They'd soon learn from that mistake and the following year it slid to the 27th for a Tenerife-based challenge. Whether you loved or hated "Changing Rooms" it represented a sea-change in the major channels realing they could get decent viewers much cheaper than if they tried a risky new sitcom or entertainment format. By the time it came to an end in 2004 the team had stencilled and spackled pretty much everything they could think of meaning it would be just boring and representing a lack of any good new ideas if it carried on… which is probably why it returned to Channel 4 in 2021. ITHANGYAW.

Tuesday, 31st December, 1996

9.50pm: Siegfried and Roy: The Magic and Mystery (BBC Two)

"They have been called the 'Liberaces of magic'…"

Anyone who might be familiar with illusionist goons Siegfried and Roy will have a good idea what to expect when the pair are given their own hour special. And thus an opening scroll reads *"these are the visions and fantasies of Siegfried and Roy..."* over footage of a moonlit snowy hill prowled by tigers and also there's an evil queen or something. With Roy's death, it might seem a bit unpleasant to mercilessly mock his work but its legitimately impossible to take seriously as their probably impressive act is rendered pointless by a series of quirky angles and fast cutting edits. This is combined with interviews that show the magicians apparently without any self-awareness, telling us how great they are (*"ve are like fire and water, thunder and lightning"*) and how they save all the exotic creatures out of the goodness of their bank balance.

Perhaps the most frustrating moment comes when the barely magical gonks claim they're going to reveal their biggest secret only to actually then say it's that "we believe in magic". Ahhhhhh. I defy anyone not to laugh at another sequence where dancers in elaborate costumes surround muscle men yelling "SARMOTI" which apparently means "Siegfried and Roy Masters Of the Impossible" and not what I hoped "Steve At Ryman's Making Orgasm Type Indications". A scene featuring a nearly bare lady in a various magical apparatus is accompanied by 2 Unlimited's "Get Ready For This" and just screams for Gob from "Arrested Development" to walk on stage with them.

Tuesday, 31st December, 1996

10.15pm: The Bob Downe Special (ITV)

"The Australian comedian and TV host presents a mixture of comedy, music and star guests"

A proper big light entertainment bonanza with music, comedy and dancing, all performed in a huge studio. You might think Cilla or Brucie is about to walk out but instead it's a beaming orange Australian in an ugly tracksuit mumbling through a cover of "Fame". This is the vainglorious, graceless Bob Downe finally getting his bite of the apple after guest appearances on every stand up showcase going. Downe is the supposed star of the daytime series "Good Morning Murwillumbah" back home and we see a few not especially well realised clips of this throughout.

A programme like this rises and falls on its guest bookings and Downe's got an absolute doozy here to begin with as the magnificent Anthony Newley appears to sing his own composition "The Candy Man" with Laurie Holloway's orchestra then indulge in a bit of showbiz patter. He's in London to star in the musical of "Scrooge" and clearly having a ball being let back on the telly for a bit, joking about how everyone had bigger hits with his songs. With less than three years left to live, it's a pleasure to see Newley even when playing second banana to Downe who by this point has established himself as an acquired taste. Crooned versions of "Mack The Knife" and "Yeh Yeh" follow in a 'not quite straight but not funny either' manner then the pre-"SM:TV" pop stars Ant and Dec come on for some stilted jokes about "confirmed bachelors" before all three sing "Lady Marmalade" during which Ant and Dec are grinded upon by female dancers in a way that seems to say "It's okay, they're not gays, folks!" The final guest is Martine McCutcheon who gamely runs through "Don't You Want Me" and a wacky version of Dean Friedman's "Lucky Stars" inelegantly seated on beanbags.

At his peak during the retro nostalgia craving for the 1970s, Mark Trevorrow's cheesy, lounge singing creation Downe is clearly a loving parody of that era and yet here it feels like nobody can decide if this is a genuine big light entertainment show or a parody of one. For such a clearly lavish production it feels strange it went out after 10pm on New Year's Eve. ITV had given a number of starring vehicles this Christmas to popular stand up acts including

Jack Dee, Lee Evans and Jeff Green but little came of any of them and, despite the British love of all things Australian that aren't cricket based, Downe's strange throwback hour was no exception.

Wednesday, 1st January, 1997

9.20pm: The Tony Ferrino Phenomenon (BBC Two)

"He is also widely adored across Brazil and Iraq. He has won Denmark's coveted Golden Throat award a record twice."

10.25pm: Cows (Channel 4)

"The Johnson family are cows and they have a problem."

And we start 1997 with two fairly-overlooked flops made by Pozzitive Television, however one is definitely a lot more fun than the other. Not dissimilar to Bob Downe, "The Tony Ferrino Phenomenon" presents a world where light entertainment never died and the Europop likes of Julio Iglesias and Demis Roussos ruled all that they surveyed. This was Steve Coogan's new character and here he gets to sing, dance and present a portrait of a slightly sketchy entertainer who was big in Europe, can't pronounce "phenomenon" and you definitely shouldn't cross.

Launched with a huge fanfare with an in-character appearance on "Clive Anderson's All Talk", expectations were through the roof before he'd even opened his mouth. There was an album readied for release and a single – the double A-side cover of the Tom Jones favourite "Help Yourself" and the wonderful original "Bigamy at Christmas" – which led him to cropping up in unlikely locations such as The Royal Variety Performance, "The National Lottery Live" and kids magazine show "Live and Kicking". Had Ferrino been played by a more unknown comic like Mark Trevorrow he might have stood a chance but by the time this show aired the single had already flopped and the hype bubble was long burst which is a bloody shame because there is tons to enjoy in both this and the spoof interview "Introducing Tony Ferrino: Who and Why?" which followed two days later.

The songs, co-written with Steve's former indie pop star brother Martin and - Glenn Ponder himself - Steve Brown are spot on pastiches of whatever needs it. "Sunday For Me" is a late-60s psych-pop number, "Stuttering Sadie From Stuttgart" is perfect dreadful early 80s novelty Euro hit and Kim Wilde joins him for the appropriately over-wrought duet ballad "Short-Term Affair" but the real stand-out is the fake West End musical showstopper "Silence Of The Lambs" based on the 1991 thriller (*"Goodness me the blood looks flesh/ Golly what a hungry feller! / Hannibal's eatin' human flesh!"*) featuring choreography by the soon to be massively famous Bruno Tonioli.

There's a lot of attention gone into faking clips of Ferrino's troubled and troubling past such as his traditional folk group with his (now dead, almost certainly by his own hand) brothers Peron and Herod singing about "fish and seafood" on one of those strange European variety shows and the 1980 Eurovision winning entry "Papa Bendi" which comes complete with a damning Terry Wogan voiceover. With a script from Coogan and Henry Normal, this is a character that proved that while Alan Partridge and Paul Calf were a tough act to follow, there was a lot more in Steve's toolbox just waiting to be discovered.

After all that praise for Ferrino, you'd assume I'd now turn on the Eddie Izzard co-written sitcom "Cows" with boredom and disdain. And you'd be entirely correct. Spoken about in revolutionary terms by Izzard for years before and rarely by anyone since, this is basically an ok sketch stretched out beyond reason with the main jokes being how cows are slightly different to humans – they have a barn conversion home but they converted it from a house to a barn! They eat chips for breakfast! They watch porn as "nature programmes"!

The briefest of back story is provided by the title sequence with spinning newspapers and fake news clips showing cows rising up to fight for freedom[47]. The cow characters are modern, naïve and fun-loving but don't really have much else to them. The plot of this fifty minute pilot is basically two episodes glued together with a human / cow wedding in the first half and the head of the household running for parliament in the second with neither story feeling like it belongs next to the other. You can hear Izzard's voice[48] in the characters but with him not in the cast, it feels a bit like a tribute act than original creation. Considering the high profile cast featuring Pam Ferris, James Fleet and Patrick Barlow under ugly latex cow masks and Sally Phillips as the token human, it's just a lot of nothing and impossible to imagine going any further than this solitary pilot. Moo-ve on already….

---

[47] Initial press reports suggested the series would focus on the cow revolution of the 1930s which is barely touched upon here

[48] He wrote this script with Nick Whitby who would later pen the "Smack The Pony" spin-off film "Gladiatress" which can be best described as never described.

1997

Highest Rated Programme: Comedy reigns supreme with "One Foot In The Grave", Men Behaving Badly" and "They Think It's All Over" in the top five 15.5m watching Gary and Tony at 10:20pm. As ITV were airing a repeat of "The Bare Necessities" (a drama not dissimilar to that year's cinema smash "The Full Monty"), Channel 4 had opera and BBC2 was just settling into a French subtitled historical film, it could be said the competition wasn't terribly strong, mind. Only soaps made it in for ITV with 12.6m saw Kevin and Sally reuniting on Corrie. Aww…

Big Films on the BBC: Is it truly Christmas before Harrison Ford has bellowed at a terrorist? "Clear and Present Danger" ticks that box for. Equally terrifying is the live-action "The Flintstones" which pops up on Christmas Day ahead of the 1994 surprise hit "The Mask". Best of the bunch is probably James Cameron's "True Lies" although timing a film to finish at 12:35am is madness, Boxing Day or not! It's back to the high-brow for BBC Two with the 1995 adaptation of Puccini's "Madame Butterfly", French historical drama "La Reine Margot", Ken Russell's "Women In Love", the 1994 adaptation of "The Browning Version" and "The Umbrellas of Cherbourg".

Big Films on ITV: Very few premieres again as Sky continued to swoop in and grab stuff years before terrestrial got a sniff. ITV make the most of it with comfortable favourites "Pretty Woman", "Gremlins", "Close Encounters of The Third Kind" and "A League of Their Own". They do hold the trump card still as "The Muppet Christmas Carol" takes pride of place against the Bedrock-based bollocks on the other side. Later "Home Alone 2:

Lost In New York" struggles to live up to its predecessor. And not just because of the horrible orange-faced git appearing in a cameo within.

Big Films on Channel 4: To tie in with their 15th birthday celebrations, there's a season of 'Film on Four' premieres including 1996's "A Midsummer Night's Dream" and Julianne Moore in the Todd Haynes drama "Safe". Fans of biting people on the mush and that will be more into the late night "Blood Lust" run of vampire films took in everything from "Zoltan…Hound of Dracula" to Kathryn Bigelow's "Near Dark" and the ridiculous George Hamilton spoof "Love at First Bite".

Big Films on Channel 5: They've got to start somewhere and we've got…oh god, "Michael Jackson's Moonwalker". Ouch. Boxing Night upped the stakes with a double bill of "Gone With The Wind and "The Happy Hooker". Because Channel 5 in 1997.

Oh That Queen's Speech: A historical year addressing both the recent death of Diana and her golden wedding anniversary. Its also the first Christmas message produced by ITN who would be added into the production rotation of Maj Messages from this point. The fact that the Beeb, who previously had the monopoly, had made that tell-all "Panorama" interview was definitely nothing to do with the decision. No. The 1997 speech was also the first to go out on the web so people of the world can revel in the glory of a stuttering 0.5MB Real Media video file that takes 2 days to download. Just what she would've wanted.

For The Kids: "Harry and The Hendersons"! "Happy Days"! "Dennis"! "Mighty Max"! "Yakky Duck"! "North and South on Tour"! "The Adventures of the Garden Fairies"! Stuff that, stay in bed until the double bill of "The Monkees" and "Eerie Indiana" on Channel 4 from half 11. Then go back to bed.

The Pops: The Girl Power continues with regular hosts Zoë Ball, Jayne Middlemiss and Jo Whiley introducing an oddly flat edition of "Top Of The Pops" despite a thoroughly eccentric and interesting year for pop. And so we get Texas, Eternal, Shola Ama, Sarah Brightman & Andrea Bocelli and a bloody megamix from Sash! A repeat appearance from Chumbawamba livens things up and the nation gets to pull their sleeves over their hands and do the "Torn" dance together with Natalie Imbruglia. And of course we all get to enjoy that great Elton John chart topper from September '97 – erm, "Something About The Way You Look Tonight". The Spice Girls are number one again and would reappear on ITV for "Spice Up Your Christmas" a gig bookended by the Spicers checking in from a fittingly OTT living room dressed with gifts, candles and a big tree. Sadly there's only room for four on the sofa so poor Mel C has to sit on the floor. When asked what they love about the Christmas period Emma Bunton talks in sickeningly cute detail about loving to see kids opening gifts at Christmas but Mel B just loves the parties. Victoria just wants quality time in Britain (which is presumably why she buggered off to Los Angeles for the best part of a decade), Mel C talks about the homeless and unfortunate, and Geri plugs their surprisingly decent new film "Spice World: The Movie" which just so happens to be released the following day. By the relatively short time the film took to come to TV, it had all gone a bit wrong. Remember them this way: pulling an oversized cracker and making Mel C sit on the floor. I said 'sit'.

Radio Times Cover: Another Santa but in a more jazzy style as a Snowman and a Robin pull a cracker. Still £1.50 and as for the films… well you'd best hope your copy still has the wrap around flap or you'd never know we're up to 900 MOVIES! 200 TV's are up for grabs too, presumably all long now dead or smashed by a crane.

TV Times Cover: Happy Tubby Christmas! Yes, for the second year running the TV Times has gone with a BBC show for the cover although admittedly there was little escaping the Teletubbies in Christmas 1997. Prizes "galore" are promised. And still flippin' £1.20!

New Year's Daze: There's Angus! There's Hogmanay Live! There's Jools! There's…wait, some actual effort from ITV? "Anthea Turner and Phillip Schofield are joined by 180,000 people in Edinburgh for the UK's biggest street party". And to prove it they've invited Texas, The Saw Doctors, Fred MacAulay and Space! There's a live "TFI" and four hours of "Under The Moon", the very cult sports chat programme hosted by Danny Kelly. Channel 5 has their usual edition of "The Jack Docherty Show" even if, between dodgy signal and the level of competition, its contents will remain forever secret.

Theme Nights: A year after "Cows" collapsed, Eddie Izzard was given his own night on Channel 4 to programme because as an opening film with Jim Broadbent as Izzard's psychiatrist suggests, his ego can now only be satisfied by doing TV. And Eddie Izzard was famous for never doing TV except "The Full Wax", "Have I Got News for You", "Mondo Rosso", "TX", "Ruby", "Shooting Stars" and that French schools programme nobody can remember the name of. Despite all that it's an entertaining mix of new stuff including the mockumentary "Lust For Glorious" directed by the Comic Strip's Peter Richardson, a curious redub of German detective series "Inspector Derrick", some Speed Archaeology and an on-going Skip Watch. He similarly picked an episode of outstanding Canadian sketch comedy series "Kids In The Hall" and Woody Allen's "Sleeper" so he's fine with me.

Also: Natural History Night is back! Six more hours of condors, chimpanzees, bats, cheetahs and stoats. But no otters sadly. At the same time Channel 4 offered viewers the chance to vote for their "Fantasy Schedule" consisting of "Friends", the 'patio' episode of "Brookside", a "Cutting Edge" documentary about road rage, the Father Ted episode on the plane, "Whose Line Is It Anyway?" and the film "Shallow Grave". There's also a bunch of ancient Egyptian themed programming plus the Taylor and Burton "Cleopatra" under the heading "Day of the Pharoahs" on Two.

Wouldn't Happen Now: Channel 4 devoted most of Christmas to celebrating its past with the fifteen anniversary "Growing Up With 4" season. The same kindness would not be returned in 2002, 2007, 2012, 2017 etc…because Channel 4 is rotten now and terrified of anyone discovering it was a niche outsider channel.

New For '98: January sees the debut of oft-overlooked John Sullivan comic drama "Roger Roger", "Goodness Gracious Me", "Louis Theroux's Weird Weekends" and the 'Gladiators but with some skating in' bafflement that is "Ice Warriors". Truly something for everyone!

Is The Sound Of Music On? No, it had been shown at Easter again! Don't they know we've got a system to these things?!

Monday, 22nd December, 1997

10am: Teletubbies (BBC Two)

"Some children decorate a Christmas tree."

Despite being a pre-school programme on at 10 in the morning, by December 1997 there wasn't a Briton alive who didn't know the names of Tinky-Winky, Dipsy, Laa-Laa and Po. They were the Teletubbies and they were here to say hello. Well more "Eh oh" due to their general gibberish speech patterns. Taking place in a green and verdant utopia with a human baby-faced sun looking down, the Teletubbies are strange pudgy alien creatures with TVs in their stomachs that show videos of children trying various learning experiences. So far, so kiddie programme and yet there was something not quite right about this world for any adults sneakily watching. Maybe it was the repetition with the catchphrase "again! again!" signalling viewers were about to see the exact same short film a second time. It could've been the silly language and stoner-friendly slowness to everything.

Of course it really was just meant as a nice children's programme from Ragdoll, the company behind "Playbox", "Rosie and Jim", "Tots TV", "Brum" and, harking back to my youngest days, "Pob's Programme". There was a pleasing familiarity to it thanks to the use of Toyah Willcox, Penelope Keith and Eric Sykes as voices throughout. It was also almost exactly the same in structure every single day: the Teletubbies would come out of their dome shaped home, dance a bit, learn something new, watch a film, immediately watch it again, play around a little then the lengthy "Tubby bye bye" sequence would commence. Again! Again!

By the time this week of special Christmas programmes appeared, the ubiquity of the four colourful characters was beginning to grate ever so slightly. First there was the Simon Cowell-organised "Teletubbies Say Eh Oh!" single - a very slight extending of the theme tune - which had shot to number one and stayed in the chart for over half a year. Teletubby dolls were also causing panic in shops as insufficient supply meant anarchy in the aisles as parents grabbed at the dwindling numbers of the new fab four. Parodies of the series would show up everywhere from "The Simpsons" to "Saturday Night Live" with Harry Enfield[49] turning them into the boozy fighting "Telecockneys"

This success spread through the world - over 120 countries – and today's episode - "Christmas Tree" was the 111th of 118 episodes made in 1997 and, as you would have thought, found the fuzzy foursome getting a tree after watching some children pick and decorate a tree of their own. Whether it fixed the sadness in a post-Diana world is hard to say but the place was a damn sight more colourful and ridiculous for a time after thanks to this lot…

Monday, 22nd December, 1997

5.50pm: Ant & Dec's Geordie Christmas (Channel 4)

"Ant McPartlin and Declan Donnelly return home to Newcastle"

The Ant and Dec story is one told a hundred times, usually by them at £14.99 a throw in hardback. Whether you're a fan or not,

---

[49] Whose 1992 sketch "English For Aliens" featured some not entirely dissimilar characters with aerial heads and limited vocabulary. TREE!

thirty years of pretty much solidly being on television isn't a bad go, mind and I speak from experience as someone who grew up watching kids TV when they were highlighting the dangers of paint in eye, quietly bought a copy of their debut album "Psyche" then hid it as I hit my teens. I loved the funny and irreverent variety show "The Ant and Dec Show" and the underrated awkward phase (for them and me) of Channel 4's "Ant and Dec Unzipped". A potentially disastrous career jump back to kids' telly would follow in 1998 but before that there was one last hurrah for C4 in "Ant and Dec's Geordie Christmas".

This is the naughtier, more laddish version of the duo (*"Goodwill to all men? Does that mean we can still throw snowballs at lasses then?"*) but thankfully they're a lot more charming than they'd been on "The Bob Downe Special" the year before. Recorded "as live" from a cruise boat on the Tyne and featuring the spectacular Kenickie as a house band, it's like "TFI Friday" hosted by a teenage Reeves and Mortimer. A blend of daft sketches, interviews and Evans-like stunts follow such as flinging a giant pie over the River Tyne to Gateshead, seeing what Joe Pasquale sounds like on helium, kicking flaming Christmas puddings and a man who claims he can win a tug of war with the boat being driven by Maureen from recent docusoap hit "Driving School" because its 1997. Other guests include Rowland Rivron as the Ghost of Christmas Past with some deeply unpleasant old timey traditions, Aled Jones singing rewritten comedy carols, Roy Wood singing that song again and some footballsmen who come on for a Geordie quiz judged by Peter Beardsley who presumably snuck out between cooking eggs. It's a really exuberant funny half hour - the pair reading out "bad things to have on your Christmas cards" including tanks, bums, cheese and dogs 'cementing their relationship' made me actually choke with laughter - fronted by a ready for prime-time Ant and Dec with scripts from the people who would follow them to "SM:TV" - Gary Howe, Richard Preddy and Dean Wilkinson.

Monday 22nd December, 1997

11.15pm: Stella Street (BBC Two)

"The first of ten short satirical dramas starring John Sessions and Phil Cornwell as myriad celebrities who have retired to Surbiton."

Both a single joke premise and one of the most inventive comedies of the decade, "Stella Street" presented a world where the plotline 'Al Pacino is in a hurry to catch a cab but Jimmy Hill hopes to borrow a cake nozzle from him before he goes' not only makes perfect sense but you're excited to see how it works out. This is entirely down to the performances by writers and creators John Sessions and Phil Cornwell who along with director Peter Richardson took basic impersonations of celebrities and curved them into realistic characters living lives of calm domesticity. Our guide to proceedings is a 60s-era Michael Caine (Cornwell) who in this episode is preparing lunch for cantankerous elderly resident Mrs Huggett (Sessions) and on the way introduces us to our cast of players. Jack Nicholson (Cornwell) is waiting for a lady visitor (*"he's like a rat up a drainpipe… mind you he does nice apple crumble*") as Jimmy Hill (Cornwell) is in the park playing football trying to avoid the scary Joe Pesci (Sessions) doing some Mafioso style 'gardening' and a waspish Dirk Bogarde (Sessions). Perhaps the series' most enduring characters were a petulant Mick Jagger (Cornwell) and constantly bombed Keith Richards (Sessions) running the corner shop. *"Remember the Man who fell to Earth? Well he landed here at No.2..."* – here's mid-70s era Bowie and he urgently needs help with his dishwasher, a plot point we'll have to wait a few episodes to follow up on due to the ten-minute length of each show.

This was another one of BBC Two's short programmes spread over Christmas week and with both the scatter-shot scheduling and general insanity the period traditionally brings it felt like a genuine treat when you stumbled across one of the episodes airing. Rarely being cruel to its subjects and done with a visibly genuine love for an older era of larger-than-life personalities, both Cornwell and Sessions were at the top of their game here. Both had been recognisable names with Cornwell breaking through as the voice of snotty alien puppet Gilbert on "Get Fresh". Despite never becoming a mainstream success, the madness and mundanity of Surbiton's finest featured highly in the obituaries after John Sessions' passing in November 2020. Always a great improviser, actor and wit his ubiquity and unashamed lofty reference points in the early 90s did mark him out as a target for those who couldn't see the appeal. The fast-paced, clever and yet very silly "Stella Street" was an accessible way in for everybody as the recognisable impersonations allowed the creative team to get stranger and build in more narrative as the series progressed.

Here's looking at you, Mrs Huggett…

Wednesday, 24th December, 1997

7.50pm: A Perfect Day for Christmas (BBC One)

"A Christmas Eve transmission of the BBC's promotional video"

Created to promote the vast array of music the BBC broadcast on its various telly and radio stations, most people of a certain age will remember this all-star cover version of Lou Reed's beautiful 1972 paean to love and definitely not heroin which had never been a single in its own right but had returned to public attention when featured in 1996's hit movie "Trainspotting". Which is probably is about heroin now I think about it. Despite this druggy new context, the BBC went along with it and managed to hook an impressive array of artists to take a line or two each with everything from opera to trip-hop covered. Reed himself is here flanked by the original record's producer David Bowie whilst eclectic mix including Elton John, Evan Dando, Bono, Boyzone (apparently dressed in bin bags) bring their unique styles to the record. The repetition of the advert meant it became a record that many started to impersonate every time it came on TV with baritone Thomas Allen's *"You just keeeeeeeeep me hanging on"*, Shane McGowan's obliviously off key *"its such funnnnnnn"* and Heather Small's vaguely threatening *"YOU'RE GOING TO REEEAAAP!"* particular favourites to copy.

It absolutely should not work as a record with soprano Lesley Garrett next to reggae legend Burning Spear then a sax solo by Courtney Pine and yet it's a surprising triumph touching upon a number of genres but never tipping over into sickly sentimentality. A release in aid of Children In Need popped up in November

1997 and stayed at number one for three weeks in the UK[50], eventually raising over £2 million. However, if you want to hear it again legally, you might have to text in to Ken Bruce as the fiddly contracts for getting all those acts on one record means it has never made it to the digital age.

Thursday, 25th December, 1997

9pm: Seinfeld (Sky One)

Celebrating the holidays but rarely with a smile on its face, "Seinfeld" was at this point in its ninth and final season. With co-creator Larry David gone it's generally considered by fans to be an uneven series but there were some highlights such as this holiday episode "The Strike" which popularised "Festivus", an event the put upon George's cantankerous father had invented[51] as an alternative to Christmas (*"I find tinsel distracting"*) for December 23rd. The plot mixes in the history of "a Festivus for the rest of us" with George making up a fictional charity, Elaine tracking her lost sub sandwich card and usual layabout dreamer Kramer's returning to the bagel shop he worked at after a twelve-year boycott. Bryan Cranston appears as recurring "Dentist to the

---

[50] And seven weeks in Ireland with it even holding off the Spice Girls for Christmas Number One there!

[51] It was actually invented by writer Daniel O'Keefe in the sixties as a fun way to commemorate the anniversary of his first date with future wife Deborah. His son Dan would write this episode with his family's blessing and would later wrote a book on the subject entitled "The Real Festivus".

Stars" Tim Whatley alongside a denim-vest wearing Kevin McDonald from "Kids in the Hall" who is always a delight to see in anything. A joke about a woman being a "two-face" vacillating between looking good or bad has dated horribly but lines like "Stop crying and fight your father" continue to represent the series perfectly. Alongside "Friends" and "ER", "Seinfeld" was the US hit of the decade, rising from poor ratings and constant fear of cancellation to become the most watched programme in the country with over 22 million at its peak. Here in the UK however it just never quite took off despite BBC Two giving it several decent slots[52] to only cult success. It would eventually find a common bedfellow in "The Larry Sanders Show" with both airing in a post "Newsnight" slot for a number of years, eventually reaching the end three years after the cast had said their goodbyes in America.

Thursday, 25th December, 1997

10.20pm: Men Behaving Badly (BBC One)

"A day spent lying in front of the telly in a self-induced coma."

Another slow-burner sitcom that eventually exploded around its fourth series, "Men Behaving Badly" was the grubby equivalent to "Seinfeld" in many ways with this episode in particular feeling like it follows Jerry and co.'s "show about nothing" mantra. Not that

---

[52] Initially 9pm on Wednesdays in late 1993 then Saturday around 10pm. BBC Two would finally get to "The Strike" in October 2001.

this is necessarily a bad thing as we're spared any convoluted plotlines about bad Christmas trees or horrid Aunties turning up uninvited. Instead we spend a day as childless and childish people would do - sleeping late, feigning pleasure at crap gifts, going to the pub, drinking too much, burning the turkey and going back to bed. So we know how seasonal sitcoms are supposed to look the episode starts with a scene straight out of a Victorian Christmas card featuring carol singers, snow and big shiny presents with huge bows. The reality is then presented as a desperate Gary (Martin Clunes) goes on a Christmas Eve present search and a very drunk Tony (Neil Morrissey) attempts to snog everything including a dog and his own reflection. We'll cut back to the ideal Christmas tableau throughout the episode even if it's mostly used as an admittedly excellent excuse for some Morrissey pratfalls.

Containing some nice observational humour and a number of really funny lines (Gary telling the others when seeing he's got Tony a drum kit: "*You should be grateful, he wanted an otter!*") it's surprising how the intervening years have changed my opinions of the characters. Both easily exhausted by the world, Gary and Dorothy (Caroline Quentin) seem more suited together than I'd remembered while the character of Tony is definitely a lot more grating although admittedly he is turned up to 11 here after finally convincing Leslie Ash's Deborah to go out with him after five series. It's a low key affair featuring just the main four cast members discussing various aspects of Christmas[53]. The one thing

[53] The only other character with any real screen time is John Thomson's odd landlord Ken, a later addition to the cast, who he feels like he's been dropped in from a very different series

they don't do in fact is turn on the television as the Radio Times said they would![54] Despite the passing years, it remains incredibly rude and I still can't believe it went out on Christmas night as the BBC struggled to find a replacement for its rapidly depleting catalogue of sitcoms. And that's before we even get to the following years special which would top it with sticky tissues to spare...

Thursday, 25th December, 1997

11.40pm: I Hate Christmas Too! (BBC One)

"A contemporary Christmas fable"

"Blue Christmas" by Elvis is playing and Peter Capaldi is throwing a stuffed toy in a bin. I think he might be upset about something? Suddenly the vision of a WWI soldier (Samuel West) appears to show him how the war was actually bad and not good like you thought, even when they had a lovely ceasefire kick about. This was 1997's penance for still being up late on Christmas night and with the former resident of the five minute slightly-religious bit John Wells not in the best health they still needed to make people feel bad about themselves somehow. And so we learn the valuable lesson "you're not allowed to be sad because there was a war once". Thanks war ghost!

---

[54] The episode being recorded in late November would have no doubt foxed the RT and its presumably ridiculous deadlines.

Friday, 26th December, 1997

5.25pm: The Light Lunch Cardigan Christmas (Channel 4)

"Plenty of party tricks and games when Mel and Sue are joined for tea by Vic Reeves, Bob Mortimer and Ulrika Jonsson…"

Scheduled at half 12 and introducing the world to the Mel (the mumsy, excitable one) and Sue (the cool, deadpan one) double act, "Light Lunch" was for a time one of those programmes you felt only you were watching with a 'chatting 'n' cooking' format that has been ripped off by pretty much any live weekend programme that's not about balls or Jesus. Comedians first, becoming presenters wasn't the smoothest of transitions but that's part of the reason their growing army of fans started to love them. Ulrika Jonsson comes out first to produce that episode's main meal - potatoes and lager - before Vic and Bob try and eat it. Usually good value on chat shows (Bob announcing he got edible knickers for Christmas is very on form) they're not on their best behaviour here as they constantly needle a stony faced Ulrika. Pudding is a chocolate log (*"Vic, what is chocolate?", "I don't know but I dig it out of something"*) a la R&M which they decorate with cutlery (*"Don't scrape it! it's not a lady's face!"*)

Christmas crackers featuring horoscopes done by Russell Grant revealing Vic is going to try a different role, Ulrika is going to have a turbulent year and Bob needs to stay sweet (he also needs to "hide his bobble hat as it will link him to a terrible crime", These may not be Russell's exact words, mind.) Paying tribute to Shooting Stars' "Dove from Above", the final game is "The Quirky Turkey from Albuquerque Whose Past Is A Little Bit

Murky...From Over There" and features the unlikely quartet of Holly Johnson, Lynne Perrie, Gordon Burns (Ulrika: *"Gordon's a granddad"*, Gordon: *"You're not allowed to say that on television!"*, Bob: *"Okay, Gordon's a murderer!"*) and Carol Smillie ringing in with questions. With only two months left before an awkward, truncated version was moved to 6pm as "Late Lunch", this wasn't Mel and Sue at their best but definitely at their most interesting and light.

Friday, 26th December, 1997

9pm: Walker, Texas Ranger (Sky One)

"Walker tells a ranger's version of A Christmas Carol"

Co-created by future Oscar winner (and, more importantly, the bloke behind "Due South") Paul Haggis, "Walker, Texas Ranger" has Chuck Norris in it and that's pretty much all you need to know. He punches, he kicks, he has a tragic backstory and was in 'Nam. You know the drill. If I told you this episode started with an orphanage Christmas party (we know, they've a sign up) in a bar and has a very high-trousered Walker pestered for a seasonal tale, despite one stubborn kid saying Christmas stinks, would you believe me? Let's ask the man in the risible trews: *"Back in 1876, there was a ranger named Hayes Cooper who was an orphan just like you kids..."* Cue flashback...

This is easy TV for an older generation but if the image of Chuck Norris shooting a bad guy in the ass doesn't make you smile, there's no Christmas spirit in you…

Saturday, 27th December, 1997

2.00pm: CITV Awards (ITV)

"Neil Buchanan presents the seasonal show."

It's startling the difference a year or two makes. At one point I would've been all over the CITV schedule knowing every programme from "Alias The Jester" to "ZZZap!" even if it was just so I knew what to avoid. But by 1996 I was nearly seventeen and clearly above such childish things like "The CITV Awards" preferring more sophisticated entertainment like "Sunnyside Farm" and "The Ten Minute Free Bit On The Adult Channel". So this ceremony - the third and final one apparently - escaped my attention at the time meaning I missed "Name That Toon" (nope, sorry) winning "Most Fun Show" and Lisa Riley saying she's "gagging to meet" Ronan Keating and Peter Andre.

Tongue removed from cheek, it's a shame CITV aren't able to (or wont) do stuff like this strange amalgam of sitcom, pantomime and award show anymore. Our host is 'Santa' Neil Buchanan who rhymes every line because the setting for the ceremony is Pantoland (*"Timmy Mallet and Mark Speight / I tell you now this shows just great!"*) To give you a small taster: The evil Shane Richie and his sidekick - the kid with the plastic wig from Saturday morning series "Scratchy and Co" - upset some awful child singers so Timmy Mallet gets them dancing to "Firestarter" instead. Clearly not aimed at me aged 16 or 40, it's a reminder of the strength of ITV's youth output before it was all shuffled off to a digital channel with the minimum of effort put in throughout.

Saturday, 27th December, 1997

6.05pm: Gladiators - Celebrity Special (ITV)

"A seasonal version of the Physical-challenge show."

As I hope you've noticed by now, I've tried to pick a lot of shows that had cultural impact. Some series influenced much than came after them, others were unique and could never be replicated. And then there's "Gladiators - Celebrities vs. Jockeys" which is an episode of "Gladiators" with celebrities. And jockeys. Can a jockey be a celebrity? What makes a celebrity not a jockey? And where's Jet? The answers to none of these questions will be answered over the next hour...

First up for the celebrities is Bradley Walsh, a long way from his current beloved status, who makes an awful joke about showering with the Gladiators but has an impressive run in the tennis ball-dodging "Danger Zone". Not far behind him is a 55-year old jockey Willie Carson who makes a joke about his short stature meaning he'll be hard to catch. He is then caught within 3 seconds. After them Mark Speight (occasionally in his "Scratchy and Co" outfit), Bob Champion and Peter Scudamore. We continue to push the word "celebrity" to its most finite level as Mr Motivator takes on jockey Carl Llewellyn on that wall climbing thing, followed by Paul Ross and the incomprehensible Tony Dobbin in a battle of the century best described as "uninspiring".

In the commentary box, John Sachs says things like "She tried to pull him off", "Bradley's legendary in the business for his scoring skills", "his wife knows her Willie is just under five feet tall" and "Sam deciding to milk it over her some more" without even a giggle in his voice. Hosting the show is Ulrika Jonsson albeit a post-"Shooting Stars" Ulrika and she doesn't seem to give much of a stuff about anything with a tone that veers wildly between sassy and shitty.

For a time "Gladiators" was the biggest non-bearded thing in Saturday night entertainment with competitors becoming household names - even if those names were things like Laser, Panther and Saracen. But this special feels a bit sad, like turning up to a party that's already over.

Look away now if you don't want to see who won. (It was Jockeys.[55])

Wednesday, 31st December. 1997

10.10pm: Adam and Joe's Fourmative Years (Channel 4)

"Couch potatoes Adam Buxton and Joe Cornish scour the archives for highlights and lowlights in the channel's history."

The sort of programme that could last eight hours and you'd never get bored, Adam and Joe were growing in popularity at Channel 4 and to cement that rise they were given this one-off special to chart the journey of the fourth channel as it hit its fifteenth anniversary. Digging through the archives, they pick all sorts of long forgotten and best forgotten shows that never get mentioned on the talking head clip shows that television would soon be

[55] For all the effort they would take home a measly five grand for their charity. Even accounting for inflation, that's a bit bobbins.

dominated by. Known for their toy renditions of famous TV programmes and movies, this episode begins with a toy version of Adam and Joe in 1982 turning on the exciting new Channel 4 for the first time, seeing “Countdown” and falling asleep. This sums up the eighties era - a mix of the hugely exciting and utterly tedious – but Buxton and Cornish clearly relish the chance to talk about all this old guff with affection. There is more obvious stuff like pretentious 'art happening' “Club X” and “Mini Pops” with its inappropriately sexual pre-teen versions of current hits but we’re also treated to snippets of forgotten fare like “The Pocket Money Programme”, “Trak Trix”, “Paul Hogan's England”, and “Watch This Space”.

Regular characters the Vinyl Justice squad look at the channel's early pop output including “The Tube” “Ear Say” with the “notorious” Gary Crowley, “Whatever You Want” featuring a barely grown Wham! and the “Malibu World Disco Dance Championships 1983” with Leeeeeeeee John. Later we’re treated to the brilliant “Star Test” and its supposedly interactive chat which let celebrities like Bros or Terence Trent D'arby shine or hang themselves with their responses.

Adam's late father Nigel “BaaadDad” Buxton talks viewers through the naughtier programmes in the back catalogue such as 1986's “Naked Yoga”, the 1993 documentary “Sacred Sex” and “The Very Hot Gossip Show” featuring the Kenny Everett dancers doing much like they had on that series but with more close-ups on wiggling bums. On that same tack, the infamous “red triangle” late night ‘culture’ films are mentioned as is the channel's commitment to post-midnight experimental video art (*“There's a thin line between art and complete bollocks, see if you can guess which is which")* and "suicidally grim drama".

A treat for fans of archive telly, swearing toys and gleefully daft jokes, this is a love letter to a unique broadcasting period and a Channel 4 that's depressingly unrecognisable in its current form.

Wednesday, 31st December. 1997

11.00pm: TFI 1998 (Channel 4)

Last seen throwing frozen turkeys at people in "Don't Forget Your Toothbrush", we catch up with a very different era of Chris Evans' career now. Originally planned for a disinterested Jonathan Ross, "TFI Friday" quickly established itself as another must-watch with lots of his trademark big ideas plus the hippest guests of the day and the most in demand alternative music live. Even some of the ginger-bonced host's biggest critics couldn't deny there was something special about those first six months of TFI. However, the episode that aired over New Year 97-98 was not part of those months.

We skip the usual opening band for Chris telling a fun story about throwing up and how the little things under the toilet seat look like chipolatas. *"I'm drinking for a good cause"* says Chris to his whipping boy producer Will, *"what cause?"* he replies, *"...cause I'm an alcoholic"* comes the grim and probably truthful reply. At this point, upcoming guest and real life recovering alcoholic Frank Skinner must be sat backstage wondering why he hadn't gone on "Hogmanay Live" instead. Before him is Melinda Messenger, a model turned presenter who had experienced a wave of fame due to being funny and genuinely likeable even under the onslaught of jokes about her sizable chest.[56] It's no surprise that a year on from this she would already have her own chat show. Sadly it was on Channel 5 so nobody knew.

After her we meet people who have "made a change in 1997" which immediately sets alarm bells ringing and - yes indeed - the first person on stage had had a boob job. Producer Will promises the standard would improve and we get to meet the punky Elaine Davidson who had become the Guinness World Record holder for the most piercings[57] before it's...another woman who has had a boob job. The male winner of 1997's series of "Gladiators" is next[58] and then...oh good another boob job. Rounding off the section is someone who has had surgery in order to change gender. They're confident funny and seem comfortable in their skin, unlike Evans who doesn't know what to say so over-compensates with more babble about bosoms.

---

[56] Asked to make predictions for 1998 she says that Bentley Rhythm Ace will have a number one (their one future Top 40 entry would be 2000's ace "Theme From Gutbuster" which peaked at 29) and celeb couple Liam Gallagher and Patsy Kensit would have a baby. One of them did but singer Lisa Moorish was the mother after an affair the previous year. Kensit would eventually give birth to Lennon Gallagher in 1999.

[57] Elaine was still the most pierced woman as of 2018 with 4,225 skin piercings to her face and body.

[58] A chap named Mark Mottram who became a respected stunt coordinator on several Bond films, "Batman Begins" "Hot Fuzz", "24", "Game of Thrones" and...basically everything.

There are flashes of the old ideas factory as the crew have set up 1,998 alarm clocks set to go off at midnight so they don't miss it. Evans also has breakable stunt bottles to smash over guests' heads and maggots in his drawer for no apparent reason other than it'd probably be funny. A heavily trailed feature in the first and second parts is later dropped due to them over-running which was no bad for a programme with hardly any content. At least we've music and kicking off this 'review of 97' is Ocean Colour Scene with…a song from 1996. As if to service Evans' ego they play "The Riverboat Song" - i.e. the song that plays when anyone walks onto the set on "TFI Friday". As mild compensation they later return to perform the more recent "Hundred Mile High City". Also here is Mark Owen running through his mostly failed first attempt at solo success after Take That.

Frank Skinner's next and sets the tone with opening jokes about Gary Glitter and fancying a job on a radio station[59]. The world then freezes for a second when Evans asks if 1998 will be the year his mum is allowed to call him his real name Chris again seemingly unaware that Skinner's mother has been dead since 1989. In his bluster, he tries to blame an off-screen Danny Baker but the mood is tarred and doesn't get better when Des Lynam, at the peak of his ironic hipness, arrives to talk about a great year for sport. Leading the actual count down to midnight is the actual "Countdown" clock from Channel 4's long running quiz. Auld Lang Syne is sung (a dazed Evans seems unsure of the words)

---

[59] Referencing Evans' very recent purchasing of Virgin Radio through his Ginger Media Group. "Preferably Simon Mayo's on Radio 1" comes the punchline which is ironic considering he's spent the last decade in the old Virgin building as part of the Absolute Radio line-up...

then a pissed Ocean Colour Scene bellow "arse" over the final link and we're thankfully done bar the best bit of the evening - Chumbawamba, no doubt cursing their booking agent and wearing "One Hit Wonder" T-shirts, singing the still anthemic "Tubthumping".

Had it come the year before, this could've just about held together quite entertainingly. How TFI wobbled onto 2000 is anyone's guess although even Evans had wandered off by that point to have sex with teen pop stars and drink himself into oblivion.

And yet, weirdly, he'd be back...

1998

Highest Rated Programme: A tie at the top with "Men Behaving Badly" and "EastEnders" averaging 13.9 million and the Street not far behind with 13.5m viewers. The biggest film of the day was BBC One's "Babe" with 8.8 million.

Big Films on the BBC: Perhaps inspired by the pink porcine pal BBC One had mostly family friendly movies this year including the 1994 remake of "Miracle on 34th Street", boring ghost adventure "Casper" and further willy freeing in "Free Willy 2". The joint is considerably classed up on BBC Two who had "Casablanca" alongside Trevor Nunn's version of "Twelfth Night" in the evening and a Gary Oldman double bill with two roles based on real people - Beethoven and playwright Joe Orton - in "Immortal Beloved" and the Alan Bennett-written "Prick Up Your Ears" respectively.

Big Films on ITV: Not much to work with here either I'll be honest – "The NeverEnding Story II", Macaulay Culkin's last movie before a hormone-tastic career break "Richie Rich", diabolical Chevy Chase comedy "Man of the House" and the forgettable 1993 take on "The Three Musketeers" making up the main premieres.

Big Films on Channel 4: The Michael Frayn farce "Remember Me?" feels a very odd choice for the evening's big new release even if it does have a cast containing most of British comedy including Robert Lindsay, Rik Mayall, Brenda Blethyn and Imelda Staunton. Odd Johnny Depp comedy "Don Juan DeMarco" and another adaptation of "Little Women" are the supposed highlights while there's more late horror with the black and white "Silent Nights, Deadly Nights" season though you'd be better getting up early than going to bed late for some of the timeslots.

Big Films on Channel 5: I mean if you're asking "is Krull on?" then yes! Sunday 20th December is your destination for awkward fantasy nonsense. The main draw for night owls however is the Russ Meyer season featuring many of the sexploitation king's more watchable films including premieres of "Supervixens", "Faster, Pussycat! Kill! Kill" and "Common Law Cabin" around the midnight hour.

Oh That Queen's Speech: Prince Charles is 50! Hip hip hooray! Maybe he'll get to be king any time now! Or, at the very least, one of those new-fangled Tamagotchis. There was also footage of the Queen Mother visiting the Field of Remembrance at Westminster Abbey. Sadly not doing her trademark hully gully or any handstands.

For The Kids: Mostly the same repeats – "Sweet Valley High", "Saved by The Bell", "Moesha", some toss with Yogi Bear in etc. The channel switching appearance of "Taz-Mania" on the BBC is a welcome sight as is an 'in the ascend-ant' "SM:TV" on Boxing Day. Channel 5 also gets in on the act although they're a long way from their current pre-school domination with repeats of "The Incredible Hulk", Lassie films and 30-year-old "George of the Jungle" cartoons.

The Pops: Middlemiss has hung on to presenting duties but its Kate Thornton and Jamie Theakston hosting a legitimately odd mix of the great (All Saints, Stardust, B*Witched), the meh (LeAnn Rimes, Boyzone, Celine Dion) and the 'of its time' (Fat Les, Jane McDonald, Denise Van Outen and Johnny Vaughan) but it all potters on nicely even if the now reduced Spice Girls are number one again. They're "Live At Wembley" on ITV later ploughing through the hits as if they weren't pig sick of the lot of them. I'm sure they'd rather be watching BBC One's "Robbie Williams: For One Night Only" on Christmas night.

Radio Times Cover: A very jolly cover with Father Christmas apparently on Krypton riding one of his reindeer cowboy style and lassoing some text. And that text reads.... "1000 Movies"! And the price has gone DOWN to £1.40! Down to 3 million sales.

TV Times Cover: And now it's the bloody "Changing Rooms" cast on the cover. Don't ITV have any stars anymore?! The cover prize of £1.25 also offers us all a chance to win a Porsche and a "fantastic £26 off the latest CDs and videos". Bagsy "Alistair McGowan's Football Backchat 2", mam!

New Year's Daze: All as before on BBC One – Angus on "The End of The Year Show", Scottish celebrations with terrible guests (Frank Bruno, the McGann brothers and Sarah Brightman), a message from the Archbish and a Carry On film. Sadly its "Carry On Columbus" though. Over on Two the Hootenanny and Glastonbury highlights are still in their regular slot but leading up to them is "Mark Lamarr's New Year In" featuring the comedian doing his "I don't like things" shtick around a series of totally unrelated programmes ("The Making of Robot Wars", "The Simpsons" and a compilation of Scottish comedy from the early 80s amongst them) plus "The Rocky Horror Picture Show". ITV's New Year's Eve is also all over the place with the combined weight of "The Bill", Freddie Starr, a feature-length "Emmerdale", some "Ruth Rendell Mysteries" and a tribute to Scottish comic actor Stanley Baxter fifteen years after LWT got rid of him. Then it's over to a live party from Edinburgh with Jenny Powell and oh…John Leslie that lasts all of twenty minutes. Having taken Channel 4 into 1998 "TFI" with Chris Evans is back but only for a short best of leaving a "Eurotrash" compilation to see in midnight. Channel 5 has yet more "Night Fever" and dismal drama "Stanley and Iris".

Theme Nights: Perhaps the most perplexing of the lot as Channel 4 launch "Mini Night" – "three programmes about the UK's love affair with the Mini" – including a documentary on its designer Sir Alec Issigonis, fans and detractors talking about the car and a look at how the famous Mini chase in "The Italian Job" was done. Sadly "mini" is the operative word here as the whole thing takes up just two hours. Much grander on December 28th is BBC Two's Dance Night hosted by ballet dancer Deborah Bull and dance enthusiast Alexei Sayle. There are documentaries, new and old, on ballroom, ballet and even clubbing along with two movies devoted to the subject - the sublime "Strictly Ballroom" and "A Chorus Line".

Wouldn't Happen Now: Sky One's grubby, titillating "Christmas Uncovered" which offered a *"festive look at Christmas office parties, complete with full range of prurient misdemeanours"*. Had we not suffered enough with Fat Les' "Naughty Christmas (Goblin In The Office)" being released that year?

New For '99: Two formats launched in January 1999 – "Holby City" and the much more believable "Super League Show". BBC Two had its last gasp of throwing big money at comedy with "Bang, Bang, It's Reeves and Mortimer" and "The League of Gentlemen" combined with Stephen Poliakoff's "Shooting The Past" and the boardroom battle documentary strand "Blood On The Carpet". Outside the hard-edged police drama "The Vice", ITV has to wait until February for "That 70's Show" remake "Days Like These" for its own big comedy hit. See also the same joke for Channel 4 but replacing it with Richard Osman's "Boyz Unlimited".

Is The Sound Of Music On? Yes, BBC One had it on the 20th December at 2pm, just after "EastEnders" and a showing of its natural bedfellow – the "Bless This House" spin-off film.

Saturday, 19th December, 1998

2.30pm: An Audience with All Saints (ITV)

"The female pop quartet answers questions from fans."

Spice who? Yes, pop is a fickle game as me and Scooch know only too well. It'd been a hell of a year for All Saints with "Never Ever" starting the year and the Pointless answer "War of Nerves" ending it, plus the 9th bestselling album of 1998 which wasn't bad for an album that had come out the previous year. This Davina McColl hosted special was sadly not included in the official "An Audience With" canon unlike...um, "An Audience With Spice Girls" from the previous year. And yet they had the indecency the week prior to this to give an hour over to Simply bloody Red.

Sunday, 20th December, 1998

8.00pm: The Royal Variety Performance (BBC One)

"The Prince of Wales attends this year's show.."

Talking of the Spice Girls, they're in here as part of a typically bonkers Royal Variety line-up with Lily Savage, B*Witched, the cast of "Oklahoma!", Barry Manilow, Martine McCutcheon, Jim Tavaré, Phil Cool, Jane "Boats" McDonald, Stomp and some bloke named Peter Kay. This had been a surprisingly late showing for the Variety Performance which usually occurs towards the end of November and it was Chas' turn to go and show face. He'd already come into contact with the Fox Force Five when they performed at a 1997 charity gala for the Prince's Trust and where his cheek, according to Time magazine, was set upon by the lips of both Geri Halliwell and Mel B breaking all protocols and probably giving him a semi to boot. There'd also been rumours of both bum pattage and pinchage by the Spices but Geri later denied such an allegation. She'd clearly left a mark on the Royal as the following year he sent her a letter expressing his sadness at her leaving the Spice Girls. Sadly I don't think an offer was extended to form a supergroup.

Tuesday, 22nd December, 1998

8.30pm: Two Fat Ladies: A Caribbean Christmas (BBC Two)

"After receiving an invitation from a Jamaican polo team, Jennifer and Clarissa arrive at the Good Hope to prepare a festive feast."

And so we finally meet the biggest new phenomenon of the late 90s - the quirky celebrity chef. Of course it's not like there hadn't been cooking eccentrics before with the screeching Fanny Craddock in the 70s and the exuberant and often plastered Keith Floyd but the late 90s saw a real onslaught in the number of cookery programmes in prime-time and every single one of the hosts had some sort of gimmick. Gordon Ramsay shouted, Nigella made your downstairs go all funny, Hugh Fearnley-Whittingstall loved to get his hands dirty and Jamie Oliver was an annoying Mockney hipster git in a terrible indie band. But when it came to high level eccentricity and no-nonsense presentation there was nobody more beloved than the posh yet unpretentious Clarissa Dickson Wright and Jennifer Paterson otherwise known as the "Two Fat Ladies".

Three series in seemed as good a time to send them abroad somewhere and they duly arrive at passport control with their iconic Watsonian Jubilee motorbike and sidecar for a bit of playful checking in banter *("I have my electricity bill, will that do instead of my passport?")* that seems charmingly naïve in these post 9/11 times. Then we're off to Jamaica where jerked suckling pig, spiced bun and rum punch are on the menu. Though indubitably played up for the camera, the two cooks seem thoroughly at ease with their personalities and their intelligent, comic back and forth was nice to spend time with. It is particularly hilarious to hear them say "Rice and peas" in their well-bred accents without trying to be culturally inappropriate but the later wearing of Rasta hats would probably be skipped now.

With the incredible heat wearing them down the two sing a particularly rousing rendition of "God Rest Ye Merry Gentlemen" before Paterson suggests they go to Lapland the following Christmas. Sadly it wasn't to be as she would die suddenly in August 1999 midway through filming the fourth series of "Two Fat Ladies" aged 71. Why couldn't they have taken The Naked Chef instead?

Wednesday, 23rd December, 1998

10.30pm: Harry Hill's Christmas Sleigh Ride (Channel 4)

"Offbeat comedian Harry Hill presents a festive edition of the show with bizarre comedy, and surreal sketches."

Imagine never having seen an episode of Harry Hill's very cult sketch series and being greeted by the sight of an elderly actor on top of a tree declaring himself "the self-styled fairy king of Yule". That was Barrie Gosney and we're plunged straight into a Cliff Richard medley before an opening stand-up routine and clarinettist Acker Bilk playing Christmas carols on the comb and paper. It's a mystifying start if you're not familiar with the running jokes but for those of us who watched avidly every week, this was the sild on the cake. Hill's Channel 4 series felt like a 1970s Saturday night variety show that's fallen through a time warp with the celebrity guests swapped out for a series of odd characters like Ken Ford: the man "from the Joy of Sex books", Harry's stun-gun wielding mother or the actor Bert Kwouk who is employed as an incompetent chicken catcher. There's also traces of "The Goodies" in sections like "Harry and Burt at Home" a strange mini-sitcom featuring the Rory McGrath-obsessed lives of Hill and Kwouk who this week dress up as Mulder and Scully to question how Santa gets round the entire world in one night. Burt would rather catalogue his "Guns of Navarone" collection (*"they're all the same!" "Oh yeah, why would they show the same movie every year?"*) but Harry proposes trapping a Santa in a wheelie bin for his gifts. This again makes it feel like a series from a different era but with a very modern Dadaist twist and nothing represents that more than Ted Rogers suddenly appearing to do a 3-2-1 clue which results in Harry turning down his dream prize - some Sild. You know, sild - the canned young herring, invariably in a sauce. Siiiiiiiiiiillllld.

"You know what us cats like to do at Christmas.....SIT ON A BABY'S FACE" Ah, at least we have Stouffer the Cat, Harry's blue puppet pet who is joined by a similarly operated Baby Jesus. Babies in general are high on the agenda this episode as Hill's

Abbey National book-obsessed wife gives birth to a baby that looks suspiciously like Ken Ford before the whole cast sing "I Wish It Could Be Christmas Everyday" dressed as babies for....reasons. One of those programmes it's impossible to make people like if they don't get it, this wouldn't have the broader appeal of "TV Burp" or the equally daft "Alien Fun Capsule" but, like Frank Sidebottom, Vic and Bob or even "Monty Python's Flying Circus" before him, Hill created a world that ran on his own rules and logic and anyone brave enough to step inside was in for a sorted time. Respect due.

Friday, 25th December, 1998

1.00pm: Michael Flatley Talking with David Frost (Channel 5)

"Irish-American dancer Michael Flatley bares his soul."

Please don't.

Friday, 25th December, 1998

4pm: Jack and the Beanstalk (ITV)

"A star-studded cast of top comedians taking to the stage of the Old Vic.."

One of ITV's more inspired programming ideas, the revival of the celebrity pantomime for the small screen with scripts from one of the most in demand television writers of the time - "Men Behaving Badly" creator Simon Nye - provided a simple piece of family entertainment where established names could share screen time with up and coming, more alternative comedians. This first show "Jack In The Beanstalk" had Nye's old pal Nele Morrissey as the titular (and not dissimilar to Tony) Jack with his mother's bloomers filled by Adrian Edmondson having a ball in full Dame mode (*"you can't help being unattractive but you could be audible!"*) and his love interest Jill played by Denise Van Outen. The best lines are saved for Julie Walters as the Fairy Godmother and Paul Merton's on-screen narrator who gets to indulge his love of puns and torturous jokes. In smaller roles are Morwenna Banks as the irritating Goldilocks in the style of her "Absolutely" character the Little Girl, Griff Rhys Jones as the brilliantly named Baron Wasteland backed by his henchmen Julian Clary and Peter Serafinowicz.

The gags come thick and fast with plenty of post-modern nods to the old-fashioned nature of the format (*"Have you tried to live in a polystyrene house in the middle of a theatre? It's a nightmare!"*) although a few of the more adult bits about *"Shirt potatoes"*, Jill possibly having a girlfriend and Jack often *"tossing...and turning"* feel a bit forced. With Ade in a main role it's no surprise there's a bit of "Bottom"-style cartoon violence and there are original songs and music from the always appreciated Phil Pope.

The concept of Pantomime on television went back to 1948 but wouldn't become a staple of Christmas Day television until the 1960s when the BBC gave them pride of place beside "Billy Smart's Circus" and "Disney Time". These were one-off affairs featuring everyone who was anyone from Taby to Doddy, not to mention everyone's favourite future "Terry and June" cast member ~~Allan Cuthbertson~~ Terry Scott. They'd fizzled out in the mid-70s bar the odd kiddie-centric so this was the first Christmas Day panto within a teatime slot in a long while. Alas the sheer range of alternative distractions plus a constantly changing youth market saw a reduction in the family based activities of previous decades. I mean, who wants to watch "Dick Whittington" when you can do some smashing car murders on "Grand Theft Auto 3"? And so ITV pulled the plug after the fourth panto was broadcast on New Year's Day 2002. Not that it stopped ITV2 would repeating them to death, mind.

It had been a successful Christmas 1998 for Nye who had both this and the first of three finale episodes of "Men Behaving Badly" beginning later that night, plus more of his creations "The Last Salute", "How Do You Want Me?" and "My Wonderful Life" in the following year. Truly it was a good day to Nye hard. Sorry, I think these panto puns have gone to my head…

Sunday, 27th December, 1998

9.20pm: Ted and Ralph (BBC Two)

"A special one-off comedy based on the antics of two of the most popular characters from The Fast Show."

Given the speed and relentlessness of "The Fast Show", there were very few characters you could actively concede would have much of a story to tell outside their regular catchphrases[60]. On

[60] The under-seen Billy Bleach sitcom "Grass" starring Simon Day and "Swiss Toni" also featuring Higson would come later.

paper, the bittersweet tale of a lonely Lord of the Manor and his unreturned affection for his quiet groundskeeper Ted probably didn't jump out as a prime candidate for a feature length special.

Initially the creation of "Father Ted" writers Arthur Mathews and the other one this beautifully shot film was instead written by the title stars Charlie Higson and Paul Whitehouse and explores the chemistry and history between the two men as well as their home lives – Ted (Whitehouse) with his talkative wife (Kathy Burke) and Ralph (Higson) in an increasingly ramshackle mansion with broken plumbing and pigeons in the kitchen. His only real joy comes from his interactions with Ted yet when he finds him his flustered words bounce off the awkward gardener who doesn't believe in the two classes mingling.

When with his friends in the pub a much more relaxed and social Ted expresses his happiness with his lot unaware of the changes in his future when its discovered Ralph must marry before his 35th birthday or lose everything to his nearest relative the mad Aunt Cecilia (seen in flashback punching people through windows and exploding cows.) And by everything that means losing the one thing he actually cares about: Ted. A series of dates with several inappropriate candidates follow before the Ted is pushed to become wingman for his employer at a terrible party by a new-money estate owner. When a seemingly perfect young woman comes into their life, trouble is afoot, not least with Ralph's behaviour toward his closest friend...

In the series there was always an undercurrent of it simply being the story of a gay man in love with a straight man but this fleshes out a different thread from the sketches which show Ted filling a father figure role and this film shows short sepia flashbacks to Ralph's miserable youth with unloving and, at times, cruel parents. Many of the other "Fast Show" cast including Simon Day, Mark Williams and Arabella Weir pop up in multiple cameo roles and even Whitehouse brings back his drunken, slurring QC character Rowley Birkin (*"I'm afraid I was very, very drunk..."*) as Ralph's solicitor. There's also a small turn by Miranda Richardson who guests as a wife candidate marred by her passionate love for the Führer and Gina Bellman as a socialite with an intimate piercing. Richards Wilson and Griffiths also have a fun cameo as boorish landowners but this is Higson and Whitehouse's film and both are superb despite neither being a supposed "legit" actor. Indeed their transformation into these very real characters feels a million miles away from "Bono Estente!", "I'm an alien!" or "Cheesy peas!"

This is a gorgeous looking and very funny film with a huge heart that would've equally been at home on BBC One on Christmas night which asks the question: how do you find a partner when you've already got a soul mate? The saga of Ted and Ralph would continue in 2000's "The Last Fast Show Ever" with one of the most jubilant grin-inducing scenes of the entire series. Now about that drainage in the lower field…

Sunday, 27th December, 1998

10.35pm: The Johnny Vegas Television Show (Channel 4)

"A special one-off programme marking the television debut of Edinburgh Festival comedy star Johnny Vegas."

Aw, Johnny. He's lovely when he pops up on shows like "The Last Leg" or "Taskmaster" causing a bit of mischief, isn't he? Him and Bob Mortimer are basically the nation's naughty uncles, aren't they?

This is not that Johnny Vegas.

Before PG Tips. Before "Shooting Stars" and "Benidorm". Michael Pennington's creation is a bitter man out of time (*"Butlins Boy No.1! King of Singalongs?"*) constantly midway between laughter and tears living a cruel life that seems beyond his actual 28 years. People in his real home town of St Helens struggle with him because he's loud and aggressive screaming *"I'm not a comedian, I'm an entertainer!"* at anyone in earshot. It is the comedy of fear where you laugh because you honestly don't know what else to do. Fake archive clips show him at the one happy time in his life - as an entertainer in Skegness during the late 70s - contrasted with his miserable modern existence living in a caravan and bothering anyone who goes by. It's played with a realism that constantly fogs what is real and imagined with atypical actors interacting with Johnny in a naturalistic way. *"I'm preaching the word and the word is entertainment!"* You can imagine being one of those early audiences sat rigid with fear and yet unable to stop laughing at this torrent of sadness.

Channel 4 would work with Vegas again in 2005 when "18 Stone of Idiot" premiered. Slightly refined but no less manic, Johnny was still an outsider only now he was alarming celebrity guests like Elvis Costello, David Soul and Ray Winstone. Pennington with co-writer Tony Pitts purposely set out to make a show so ugly, violent and unhinged that they wouldn't possibly get a second series from Four. And, true to their plan, they did not.

Wednesday, 30th December, 1998

8.00pm: Buffy the Vampire Slayer (BBC Two)

"A feature-length pilot, starting a series of a comedy fantasy drama with bite."

A series that I associate more with the following decade yet made its debut appearance in this surprisingly respectable timeslot. Buffy was a smart, literate fast paced action comedy that allowed creator Joss Whedon to reinvent teen dramas as modern thrillers with characters who spoke like they were in 1940s screwball comedies. These were characters that also grew out of their initial simple roles and developed into more realistic, if still heavy on the riffing, humans and / or the undead. Not that I watched this pilot at the time. I mean, it was that stupid Luke Perry movie from the early 90s, wasn't it? Also it was my 18th birthday. Although if I'd known how much havoc Alyson Hannigan was going to play with my hormones for the next decade, maybe I would've.

Wednesday, 30th December, 1998

10pm: You Are Here (Channel 4)

"Dark comedy set in a remote English village named Here."

A dark comedy about people living in a strange fictional village not on any maps? Sounds familiar. It even starts on some Royston

Vasey-style moors but "You Are Here" actually beat "The League of Gentlemen" to screen by a whole 12 days, even if doesn't have to that series' impact. In fact, despite being sold as a dark comedy, "You Are Here" is more a comedy soap opera in the style of "Mary Hartman, Mary Hartman" or indeed "Soap" with dramatic sting music over scene transitions and over the top characters like Paul Kaye's psychotic suspended DI Lindsay de Paul or Matt Lucas' peculiar Pat Magnet who owns the small village of Here which in this one-off pilot has just been sold as land for a giant prison.. The support cast are brilliant with Nigel Planer, Kate Robbins, Peter Serafinowicz, Eddie Marsan, John Thomson, Paul Putner, Sally Phillips and Keith Allen who appears alongside his 12 year old son Alfie.

No series would follow even with script co-written by Lucas, David Walliams, "Friday Night Dinner" creator Robert Popper, future producing supremo Mark Freeland and journalist Jon Ronson. Although their voice is strong throughout, it's not as outright comic as some of Lucas and Walliams' later work but there's definite potential in the weird comedy melodrama style that "Green Wing" would later be applauded for six years later. It seemed for a time that Lucas and Walliams would always struggle to break through into television. A series they pitched about a spoof boy band named "Boyz Unlimited" would make it to Channel 4 in 1999 but without them attached having been left out of the pitch by their co-writer - some nobody called Richard Osman.

1999

Highest Rated Programme: And, as we dangle helplessly over the decade's end over the uncertainty of the future, it's all change on Christmas Day with ITV taking five of the top ten slots including the most watched programme for "Coronation Street" where 14.7 million watched Martin Platt have a bit of a fumble with a lady who was not his wife at work. Two editions of "Who Wants To Be A Millionaire", "Emmerdale" and the horrendously unseasonal "A Touch of Frost" also did the business for the third button. The BBC managed second place with "The Vicar of Dibley" bringing 12.4m in time for Alice to give birth during the nativity. Its thin gruel though and with no big comedy hits on the horizon, a very uncertain future approached....

Big Films on the BBC: It's an action packed festmas over on One with first showings of Michael Mann's epic "Heat", comic book adaptation "The Phantom" and Tom Cruise in one of the less memorable "Mission: Impossible" films in the franchise… erm, "Mission: Impossible". A strong Christmas Day double bill of "Jumanji" and "James and The Giant Peach" would strangely underperform thanks in part to digital TV and the video market now being so huge that both movies were old hat to the nation's kids by Christmas 1999. Another mix of enjoyable old chestnuts and worthy smaller films made up BBC Two's holiday season with the charming comedy "The Truth About Cats and Dogs", Hal Hartley's darkly comic PJ Harvey-starring "The Book of Life" and the bonkers techno-thriller "Strange Days" provide a pleasant change of pace. The latter two also happen to be set on New Year's Eve 1999. How uncanny…

Big Films on ITV: A recycle, rinse and repeat for a lot of films already shown by ITV in previous years with only "Ace Ventura: Pet Detective" making it into prime-time. One of the few premieres they do have – the 1991 Ethan Hawke family drama "White Fang" - is stuck out unceremoniously at 12:45am.

Big Films on Channel 4: Some very worthy stuff in the dramas "Welcome to Sarajevo", "Carla's Song", "The Disappearance of Finbar", "The Woodlanders" and "Ridicule" but nothing to set the pulse racing – unlike a late-night run of Akira Kurosawa films and some more lesser-known Godzilla spectaculars.

Big films on Channel 5: For the second year running Five had the most film premieres. The fact they were all mostly rubbish need hardly be the point! Applause for fabulously dumb comedy "Airheads" on Christmas Eve and head scratching for the Christmas Day scheduling of the 1969 sex comedy "Bob and Carol and Ted and Alice" followed by erotic thriller "Last Call". I mean I like interfering with myself as much as the next man but it's Christmas, lads. Have a night off.

Oh That Queen's Speech: Apparently there's one of those new millenniums starting, they kept that quiet! Obviously Liz is cock-a-hoop over the decade change to the noughties. Strange to imagine twenty years later she's still on the throne but long may she reign over us! Or at least until after this book is published…

For The Kids: A little bit of change for once with the new (read: made in 1995 but not shown in the UK yet) "Time Warrior" movies BBC One after kids' creepy anthology "Goosebumps" plus two cartoons older than Jesus himself - "Snorks" and "Peter Pan and The Pirates". BBC Two also had room for a full run of "Jim Henson's The Storyteller" which had been shown originally by Channel 4 a decade earlier. ITV has a bunch of "Art Attack" specials and various middling family films. Leaning into its own teen years, Channel 4 have pivoted to a more young adult schedule with a short lived sitcom from the "Saved by The Bell" bloke "Malibu, CA" and repeats of "Dawson's Creek".

The Pops: Theakston, Middlemiss and newcomer Gail Porter helm of an end of a century "Top Of The Pops" special that feels more like Sesame Street brought to you by the letters ATB and TLC plus the numbers Eiffel 65 and S Club 7. The now token alternative slot is filled by The Offspring and the nation's dads get to drop their pipes in excitement at performances by Britney, Shania and Martine McCutcheon, plus whoever Lou Bega brings out with him. "Livin' La Vida Loca" still sounds bloody marvellous though. Over on ITV, they follow up the live concerts of previous years with the Queen of Hellfire herself - Dame Thora Hird in "My Favourite Hymns". It's not even Sunday! In fact, it's a Saturday meaning Steps, Five, S Club AND Westlife on "SM:TV Live" plus a repeat of "The Pepsi Chart" on Channel 5 featuring most of the same acts in a slightly different order. There's also "Bjorn Again: Live at the Royal Albert Hall" and yet more "Night Fever" at tea time.

Radio Times Cover: Oh dear. A cover that could've only been matched by someone inhaling a cheap pack of Christmas cards and spewing them onto a sheet. There's a cherub, skaters, a sleigh, snow, puppet reindeer, teddy bear Santa, a decorative ginger tom and a crystal ball featuring the Millennium Dome (not pictured: a tiny screen showing a tinier "Blackadder Back And Forth") and the year 2000. All these extra millennial party ideas have however put the price back up to £1.50!

TV Times Cover: Back to a slightly sinister Santa bidding the reader to shush. Whether he's trying to keep the prize Porsche to himself or the fact it's gone up to £1.30, I can't say. But the headline "SKI THE MILLENNIUM!" takes the prize for most 'mean nothing' phrase yet.

New Year's Daze: ITV remember they have qualified "New Year's Man" Clive James on hand and duly give him the two-hour special "A Night of 1,000 Years" …on December 30th, where Jools and his Hootenanny also find themselves due to the all-out trousers to the floor live celebrations each channel had planned. BBC One broadcast the 28-hour "2000 Today" but ITV stuck with just 70 minutes in "Countdown 2000". Channel 4's newest star took over New Year for the no doubt quite rude "FY2K: Graham Norton Live" followed by "The Biggest Breakfast Ever", an eight and a half hour edition of the briefly back on form morning show with Liza Tarbuck and Johnny Vaughan. And as for Channel 5, you know they went with a four hour edition of "Night Fever" before a showing of "Emmanuelle". A cruder person would label that "Suggs and jugs". But not me. No.

Theme Nights: The theme of every channel by this point is "LOOK A MILLENNIUM!" but BBC Two do squeak in a half arsed "Nineties Night" on the 31st with a TOTP2 special, a repeat of "Gimme Gimme Gimme" and "Goodbye To The Nineties", an "affectionate look at the highs and lows of the last ten years". I bet it doesn't mention "Christmas Cluedo" though!

Wouldn't Happen Now: Lee and Herring's 1995 live video on Paramount Comedy Channel was a strange choice for Christmas night although it's still more festive than "A Touch of Frost".

New For '00: The big event was the all new "people stuck on island" BBC reality TV series "Castaway 2000" designed to air throughout the year to huge acclaim…as long as no other competing reality programmes appear and make people realise how boring and Ben Fogle-filled it was…

Is The Sound Of Music On? Excerpts from it were performed on Radio 3 on December 30th if that helps? Otherwise the Nazis win again! Boooooooooooooo!

Monday, 20th December, 1999

9.50am: B*Witched Christmas Special (ITV)

"Music documentary following the chart-topping all-girl group on tour in the UK. Featuring interviews and glimpses backstage."

Capturing the band just as their new single had limped in at 13 pretty much ending their chart career, this is a Star Test-style "confessional" with the girls selecting on screen questions in what we're to assume are their very real life own bedrooms. Because this is being broadcast some...ten hours before the watershed these stories don't creep past an admission of snoring and *"Keavy has a passion for funny socks".*[61]

With four number ones and two albums in just over a year it's plain to see the girls are exhausted and plastering on a grin for both the cameras and host Josie D'Arby. This is most evident when they're asked to watch their videography and can't help noting all the horrible things about making them, like being stuck in a harness for 17 hours *("You won't be making Supergirl The Sequel then!"* says a clearly non-plussed D'Arby.) And this is stuff they've done barely a year prior. None of it seems fun. It's a genuine shame as they were a breath of fresh air in the pop world when the denim-clad twins Edele and Keavy Lynch, Lindsay Armaou and Sinéad O'Carroll arrived with the insanely catchy "C'est La Vie" in May 1998. The follow up "Rollercoaster" is almost as good although the next two are ballads and a bit less exciting. Despite

---

[61] Sex-type people may note that with a fake computer chat graphic on screen throughout it's like a very specific sort of OnlyFans feed. Perhaps "People Who Look Like Their Da"?

being clearly ready for a long nap, the four-piece are still funny and self-effacing, the world always needs pop stars with personality.

Tuesday, 21st December, 1999

7.30pm: Massive Landmarks of the 20th Century (Channel 4)

"A disturbing wind of change threatens to alter the world for ever and it's clear the First World War is on its way..."

The works of the great Desmond Olivier Dingle have graced television and radio for nearly forty years now and still no-one has come close to an actin' and a performin' the words as good as what he does. Together with his theatre company of one Raymond Box he straddles the globe with his amazin' thinkin' and tributes to some of history's most fascinatin' people starting here in this first of six consecutive episodes with the death of Queen Victoria, Sigmund Freud's invention of psychoanalysis, Albert Einstein discovering everything is relative (*"relative to what?", "I've no idea!"*), the start of "the first World War" and the women's movement run by "Mrs Hanky-Pankhurst".

The invention of Patrick Barlow, Dingle and The National Theatre of Brent had a long history with Channel 4 stretching back to their interpretation of the "Messiah" in 1984 which lead to a full series "Mighty Moments From World History" the following year. In many ways they were a true representation of the era's cheap but over-sincere arts programmes Ch4 had regularly shown in their first decade and viewers could easily have mistaken it as much if they were a bit slow on the uptakin'. It's impossible to explain why their over-laden sentences *("Good mornin' Mr Gilbert O'Sullivan!", "Oh how lovely my husband Archduke Franz Ferdinand!")*, aitch droppin' speech patterns and minimal costume changes (usually hats and facial hair over their regular suits) are so funny but they never ever fail to have me in stitches. It's the comedy of awkwardness and ego - Dingle couldn't even begin to compute the idea that he could be wrong about some of his scripts. It's very much like an extension of Ernie Wise's "Plays Wot I Wrote" with even smaller production values and no Morecambe to puncture the pretences, although Desmond's "troupe" would generally do that for him in error. Here he is joined by the longest standing second banana of Brent, Raymond Box, played by John Ramm a simple soul who gives his all with gusto even if unrequired to do so. He had been preceded by two other assistants - the easily-confused Wallace played by Jim Broadbent and Robert Austin as the more argumentative Bernard.

Wednesday, 22nd December, 1999

9:30pm: The Flint Street Nativity (ITV)

"A festive comedy in which an all-star cast appear as young performers in a school nativity."

Now I suspect a lot of you have been wondering since buying this book "is this the same Ben Baker who gave his masterful Harlequin in the Christmas '89 performance of Panto Pronto in the hallowed gymnasium of Nessfield Primary School?" Well, I can confirm that - yes - that was indeed me. Having cruelly being passed over as Joseph in the Strong Close Nursery production of the Nativity, it was my comeback and a tour de force return to the stage... well, sports hall. An essential part of the countdown to Christmas when I was a kid, a stage production telling of the arrival of The Baby Jesus was an emotional affair with the thrill of being allowed to give up regular lessons in favour of shouting in a crown. But there were also the downsides like having to remember lines and not doing a nervous widdle in front of over eighteen massed parents grandparents and social workers. Considering all this in built drama set around the end of term Christmas play, it's a surprise nobody really nailed it until Tim Firth's brilliantly truthful "The Flint Street Nativity".

To get round the whole children acting (see above re: 'shouting in crowns') element, the cream of the comedy world have been drafted in with a jealous Gabriel played by Dervla Kirwan plotting to steal the role of Mary from Josie Lawrence. Although she's more concerned with the "tatty head" of her Joseph (Jason Hughes) who'd probably rather be playing with Frank Skinner's "A Question of Sport"-obsessed Herod or Ralf Little's Star of Bethlehem who is always getting into bother because of 'dares'. Jane Horrocks' shepherd is the over-opinionated know-all of the group *("You're not a proper donkey, you've just got a donkey's 'ead!")* and The Wise Men - a lisping Neil Morrissey, Julia Sawalha and Tony Marshall[62] - argue over have the best present for the new saviour whose head is definitely not going to fall off. It's an incredibly funny well observed play (*"He peed his leg but its ok, I mopped it up wi' a sheep..."*) with the backstage chatter revealing much about the

[62] An underrated actor who'd played Diesel in Firth's earlier series "Preston Front" and later would be better known as Nelson in "Life on Mars"

children's home lives: Stephen Tompkinson's narrator wants to learn all of his lines because his dad who "doesn't sleep in their house anymore" is coming and Shamima (Mina Anwar) cries in the toilets because she'll "get done" for not helping her social-climbing family show off to their neighbours. John Thomson's innkeeper is the eternal misunderstood rough lad who not so secretly holds a candle for Mary but Mark Addy's box-headed Donkey is perhaps the most unfortunate of the lot having an 'accident' on stage and struggling to process his grandma's death. (*"Me mum said she were old...but I looked inside her cardigan and she was only 38-40"*)

To complete the illusion of size, high camera angles and giant sets are used whilst the parent audience are kept in shadow throughout until the final act where we see they're played by the same actors as the kids. The parents are flawed, struggling and trying to get through adding just a little more realism to the script – a reflection of the commitment it took Tim Firth to gather enough real-life school anecdotes from his family and teacher friends over ten years. Having already created the wonderful comic drama "All Quiet On The Preston Front" for the BBC, Firth was by this time one of the UK's best screenwriters and would go on to script "Calendar Girls", the Madness musical "Our House", "Kinky Boots" and the fantastic "Cruise of the Gods". "The Flint Street Nativity" was never the constantly repeated treasure it should've been but has had more than a successful afterlife in stage adaptations. A wonderful way to spend an hour.

Just don't ask who wants to play Mary...

Wednesday, 22nd December, 1999

11.40pm: The 11 O'Clock Show Christmas Special (Channel 4)

"A festive celebration of comedy and music."

A celebration of dog dirt and bins more like.

From the sublime to the horrendous, I've tried to keep the subjects of this book as things I can be positive about in some way but there is little kindness I can offer to Channel4's nasty, crude topical revue show that ran from 1998 to 2000. Looking at the people that started their TV careers through it - Mackenzie Crook, Sacha Baron Cohen, Ricky Gervais, Charlie Brooker, Jon Holmes, Mitchell & Webb and Iain Lee among them - you'd assume it was a furtive breeding ground of experimental ideas and challenging comedy. It wasn't.

Lee starts his opening monologue with jokes about David Beckham being thick, Tara Palmer-Tomkinson liking drugs and Gary Glitter apparently masturbating in a card (*"Don't applaud, he's a nonce!"*) then co-host Daisy Donovan trails a sketch about drink driving with the line *"a tipple can make you a cripple"*. Good job none of the people involved did drugs, eh? Jokes about Vanessa Feltz being fat, Dudley Moore having Parkinson's disease and Christopher Reeve being disabled follow while a review of the year has them castigating Prince Phillip for his language before making jokes about Diana being bulimic and a royal website where "the Diana page crashes". How do you take the high ground with material scraping the tarmac like that?

A report on the commerciality of Christmas finds Lee visiting the Holy Land to insult local shop keepers then former Chris Morris associate Paul Garner does his best Chris Morris impression in the aforementioned drinking and driving sketch that ends with an unpleasant comedy murder. Robin Ince and Alex Lowe pop up next as John Peel and...sigh, Jimmy Savile. To be fair, both are well done if not especially funny and seem to be included for no reason than they can do the impersonations. Still at least James are there as a one-off house band for the night playing "Just Like Fred Astaire" and "Crash" from their very good album "Millionaires".

Following the break perhaps the most jaw-dropping moments occur as traditional comic Frank Carson is invited on to talk about the Irish peace process because...*shrugs*. He then proceeds to run rings around Lee and Donovan who look oddly delighted that he's playing them at their own game. After that a package featuring the "best of" Donovan's "Angel of Delight" films where she attempts to make out of touch MPs say things like sound like they're gay or like sex. Because jokes. It's a spectacularly bad segment and most of the interviewees seem totally aware of what is going on. And then we arrive at the real lowest of the low, the bargain basement of bad comedy, the bin fire's bin fire of choice Ricky Gervais as a shopping centre Santa telling children (presumably filmed separately) that they're getting nothing because they're poor or - ha ha - they're orphans! Lolle.

There's no sign of the series' breakout character Ali G who was being saved for Channel 4's "Alternative Christmas Message" on Christmas Day. In it he interviews Reverend Geoffrey Roper who handles the situation respectfully even when asked why Jesus went round with "them reindeers" and if he was like Tupac. Unlike

Gervais and many of the other people on "The 11 O'Clock Show" however the joke is always at least about the ignorance of Ali's character rather than y'know saying someone with a horrible illness deserves to be mocked.

It's satire in the loosest meaning of the word without any opinions to its thick head and no interest in anything but shock. Many of the cast have since dismissed the series including host Lee who is almost unrecognisable these days to the horrid figure presented here. Thankfully it was gone by the following Christmas although its grubby little influence filtered through the next decade especially on Channel 4 who leaned into its pranks and stitch up interviews. Merry Christmas!

Wednesday, 29th December, 1999

9.00pm: Gimme Gimme Gimme (BBC Two)

"A special of the flat-sharing comedy. New Year's Eve has finally arrived and Tom and Linda are sharing it together - drinking."

Thursday, 30th December, 1999

9.00pm: Dinnerladies (BBC One)

'The ladies are catering the firm's millennium dinner in town, but there are surprises in store."

Two very different comedies see in the coming decade. "Gimme Gimme Gimme" is a flat-share comedy about two horrible people – man-hungry bore Linda (Kathy Burke) and hopeless gay actor Tom (James Dreyfus) – being horrible to each other. I seem like

I'm on a comedy demolition course right now but it's just not a series I ever understood the appeal of with a script based less around innuendo and more just saying the rude thing to huge squawks from the audience who are clearly more on board than me. Bar dream sequences with Melinda Messenger, Simon Shepherd from "Peak Practice" and Rowland Rivron as Oscar Wilde, this is more or less a two-hander between the main characters who the actors clearly give their all to yet feel utterly wasted on.

Victoria Wood's "Dinnerladies" on the other hand is the very peak of sitcom writing with "Minnellium" coming midway through the second and final series. Every character from Thelma Barlow's social climber Dolly and her fun loving best friend Jean (Anne Reid) to Maxine Peake's sarcastic Twinkle feels tangible despite the script being smothered in jokes. Big, proper dirty woofers of gags. The story goes that each episode would be filmed twice over two nights so Wood could rewrite what hadn't worked the first time and it shows with the lines pinballing back and forth like something from an Aaron Sorkin script, all being performed by a perfect cast relishing every single moment.

This episode has the usual canteen staff being sequestered to prepare food for a big millennium knees up. Whereas many a series might show the results of that party, the action stays on the regular set and for once there is a bit of action with a baby left abandoned on the fire escape and half of Manchester seemingly on fire due to Millennium revellers. If the ending doesn't leave you a little misty eyed you are beyond a ride in my hot air balloon at the end of days.

Even though the ratings had been very good, it took a long time for the consensus on "Dinnerladies" to be overwhelmingly positive. This could be seen as a victim of circumstance as the traditional studio sitcom had started to die off through a mixture of cost-cutting and bad commissions. Wood said in interviews around the time that she had always fancied using a more naturalistic steadycam style before being convinced otherwise by a nervous BBC. While this meant that "The Royle Family" got all the credit for its genuinely different look, "Dinnerladies" remains a warm studio sitcom that feels like a cosy evening with friends.

With both airing ahead of the real minnellium…I mean, millennium they had to predict the insanity everyone predicted as we ticked over to the year 2000 with the now mocked but once a genuine concern Millennium Bug looming large and every venue announcing ridiculously priced tickets and locked doors for those without them. But what did happen? Let's put on our book ending trousers and see out this wild and wonderful decade again…

Friday, 31st December, 1999

9.15am: 2000 Today (BBC One)

"The start of biggest ever live broadcast in TV history - 28 hours of celebrations as people of the world welcome the new millennium"

Heralded by crashing music and exploding graphics this is SERIOUS TELLY FOR SERIOUS TIMES and so the Dimbleby (David model) has been deployed to give it the gravitas he usually devotes to linking to election results from Roehampton. The action starts 14 hours and 44 minutes and sixty countries are going to be filmed throughout the programme so he'll need assistance and in the studio are Peter Sissons, Fergal Keane, Gaby Roslin and...oh piss, its Parky again. Presumably millenniums were better in his time and Billy Connolly said something amusing about them to him over an episode of "The Woofits". To help us acclimatise Gaby tells us that time is a constant and they can't change things "unlike a football match...or a recorded programme". At this point it's still 9:22am, is it too early to start drinking? I mean, it's midnight somewhere...or at least it will be on the South Pacific island of Kiribati which hits the New Year first.

Music features heavily and Tim Vincent is in Cardiff where both the Manic Street Preachers AND Shaky are playing gigs, Kirsty Wark checks in from Edinburgh to tell us about something called "Hogmanay" which will soon be host to a Texas concert and their lead singer "Charleene Spittyairy". Later there's live footage from the Pyramids as a million people watch Jean Michel-Jarre playing what Michael Buerk describes as "all that Egyptian stuff", Honeyz serenade Birmingham and in Greenwich Park there's a big pop concert "in association with British Gas" including Martine McCutcheon, the Eurythmics, Bryan Ferry and sigh...Simply Red. And of course there's the Dome. Not the O2 Arena, pal. The Millennium Flipping Dome which - as we all know - cost 500 billion pounds and only showed "Blackadder Back and Forth" on a loop. Thousands flocked for its opening night where the Queen and Tony Blair watch the Archbishop of Canterbury become the opening act for The Corrs. Brilliantly the closest report to my hometown is Leeds which is represented by a roots sound system in the living room of a grotty Chapeltown terraced house.

President Yeltsin's resignation provides a bit of actual non-millennial news and some bloke named Putin is apparently favourite for his replacement. Adding more tension is a race for who will be the first baby born in the new Millennium being overseen by medical professional Nick Knowles. The potential millennium bug problems are tracked by a breathless Peter Snow as Japan experiences two failures at nuclear power plants in Isikawa and Onagawa along with several missiles being fired from Russia. As you probably can tell by the fact you're not reading this on the charred wastelands of Earth whilst eating soup made out of boiled "Threads" DVDs this wasn't a "WarGames" situation and we all got through but it's interesting to see how little we really knew what would happen when our computers blinked over to 2000. It's also testament to the months of preparation and work by IT crews all around the globe that we barely even felt the wave of change.

At half 11, we get a return of "The Two Ronnies" doing a "Ages Of Man" spin on their famous "Frost Report" class routine ("I look up to him..." etc.) with Stephen Fry taking the John Cleese role. This is a preview from an upcoming comedy special entitled "The Nearly Complete and Utter History of Everything" broadcast in two parts on 2nd and 4th January 2000 that saw various periods of time spoofed by comedy stars from the sixties to the modern day including Vic and Bob, Harry Enfield, Victoria Wood, French and Saunders, Richard Briers, Fry and Laurie, Tim Brooke-Taylor, Lenny Henry, Barbara Windsor, Hale and Pace, Jack Dee and, of course, Them Bloody Ronnies. Sadly, it wasn't very good.

There are breaks for a few programmes - the people will die if they don't get their "EastEnders" – while the morning brought "Live and Kicking" with the depressing duo of Emma Ledden and Steve Wilson' assisted' by a screeching Mr Blobby which I'm happy to say was not my first new sight of the millennium.

"2000 Today" is ridiculous, frequently filling for time and has too much Michael Parkinson on it but it's hard not to be impressed at the sheer scale of the huge production that only an organisation like the BBC could put on with such grandeur. Nearly a hundred countries simulcast some or the entire broadcast with an estimated worldwide audience of 800 million people looking on in awe and wondering if that's the bloke from "Ghostwatch". Of course things go wrong with live links dropping and the machines crashing on the National Lottery draws. But they're rare and still outdo anybody else's coverage with ITV barely bothering to go live and preferring to stick with more necessitous items like "Casper: A Spirited Beginning", "Turner and Hooch" and "Superman 2".

There's no through clear cut story to the 90s which rose and fell in both public mood and global events but through the TV we saw it all. From the first Gulf War to the Rodney King attack and the riots that followed. From the fall of Thatcher to the rise of New Labour. There was the constantly discussed and reviewed OJ Simpson trial, the cloning of Dolly the Sheep, Lorena Bobbitt's knife work, Oasis vs. Blur, the UK's return of Hong Kong, Titanic making a billion at the box office, the resurgence of the Wonderbra, peace in Northern Ireland, the Channel Tunnel, Versace's assassination, the drama of Italia '90 and Euro 96, Geri's Union Jack dress, the growth of the internet and sites like Napster threatening the music industry for the first time, Rwandan genocide, Nirvana and the shocking suicide of Kurt Cobain, Black Wednesday, a new Scottish Parliament, women priests, the boom in adult animation, Poll Tax riots, the National Lottery and the life and death of Princess Diana.

However you spent it I hope this book has provided some nice trips down memory lane and pointed out a few things you might have missed. And I am definitely, definitely DEFINITELY not writing another book about the 2000s.....okay?!

Acknowledgements

Not going to lie, this one was a toughie. The research period was a considerable step up from the 80s book where telly was happy being asleep for long periods of that decade with BBC Two and newcomer Channel 4 generally rising around 2pm. Add to that another new terrestrial channel and an increasing band of satellite stations in ever smaller fonts as the Radio and TV Times no longer have dominion over specific channels. But I got there with huge help from both Simon Tyers and Al Dupres in particular. Thanks too to Paul Abbott for his assistance with the cover and Darrell Maclaine for the best soundtrack a chap could ask for.

Thanks for support and friendship through a horrible year to Shona Brunskill, Sarah and Damian Curran with whom I probably wouldn't be here. Thanks for keeping my sanity in check on Zoom go to Phil Catterall, Christine Coulson, Garreth Hirons, Tim Worthington, Jonathan Sloman, Lorraine Ramage and Zoey Phoenix. Love also to Chris and Kylie Bate, Pete Prodge, Louis Barfe, Sean Howe, Louise Nilon, James Wallace, Tim Barker, Matt Lee, Andy Hardaker, Paul O'Brien, Jenna, Chris & the kids, Katie Kelly, Alasdair Mackenzie, Russell Hillman, Justin Lewis, Louise Gunn, Jason Heeley, Molly James, Paul Twist, Neil Miles, Jonny Mohun, John Rivers, Kirra Coates, Keir, PDT, Lisa and Andrew, all the podcast regulars and you for reading this book!

It's going to be a difficult Winter but I know we're all going to get through this one way or another. Take care of yourselves and have a very merry Christmas wherever you are!

Also By This Author

"Christmas Was Better In The 80s"

A celebration of the last great decade for Christmas telly. From the smash hits to the forgotten obscurities, it's a unique, factual yet comic look back at everything from Only Fools and Horses to Yogi Bear's All-Star Comedy Christmas Caper. It was a time before satellite or even a fourth channel to begin with! With 125 all-new mini articles, it's a fun, breezy read whether you're barmy about the box or vicarious viewer.

"Festive Double Issue: Forty Years Of Christmas TV"

A funny and factual look back at four decades of Christmas telly in the UK, good, bad and plain bizarre.

"Kill Your Television"

A love letter to all things televisual - taking in everything from ALF to Z Cars and paying tribute to the programmes, presenters, sounds and strange spin-offs that made the flashing square box in the corner of the room great.

"Ben Baker's Fun Book For The Apocalypse"

As series of silly things to do in lockdown or a very rainy day with all new quizzes, games and "procraftination" to try.

"The Comedy Cash-In Book Book"

A personal look at what made the spin-off comedy book so popular in the UK between the 1970s and 1990s. From Monty Python's exceptionally influential 'Boks' through to the unique, brilliant humour of Harry Hill taking in Morecambe and Wise, The Goodies, Kenny Everett, Saturday Night Live, The Young Ones, Lenny Henry, Smith and Jones, Reeves and Mortimer, Father Ted, Lee and Herring, The League Of Gentlemen and many more along the way. It's also got quite a lot of jokes in it. A must for anyone who likes British comedy.

"Talk About The Passion: New Adventures In Old Pop Culture"

A best of my old pop culture fanzine "TATP" plus over thirty pages of new material from myself and Tim Worthington. Viz, Godzilla, British comics, Earl Brutus, Garfield, 1986's best toys, Newsradio, Frank Sidebottom, The Beatles, Sesame Street, TV puppets and lots more feature within!

Ben Baker will return in "Christmas 2008 – I Hardly Knew Ye".